Teen Wise

"Acquire the Power of Self-Definition"

D1738264

Ms. Celeste M. Gonsalves

CMG Publishing, LLC
Hawaii
2009

Logo and Cover designed by
Naomi Midori Stafford with Midori Designs Online
www.midori-designsonline.com

Cataloging-in-Publication Data
is on file with the Library of Congress.

ISBN 978-0-615-28145-2

First Edition

Nov. 9, 2009

Dear Donna & Mark,

I hope you enjoy reading my first book and find it useful and purposeful. Please feel free to provide me with feedback. Take care.

Aloha,

Celeste M. Eyman Chun

Table of Contents

Chapter #4: The Eight Grade

Chapter #5: The Ninth Grade

Chapter #6: The Tenth Grade

Chapter #7: The Eleventh Grade

Chapter #8: The Twelfth Grade

Chapter #9: The Six Bonus Fundamentals

Chapter #10: Conclusion

Acknowledgments

First and foremost, I acknowledge with special gratitude and honored distinction my dear, sweet grandmother, Hilda Santos, for always believing in me. It was on her 86th birthday, March 26th, 2003, when I was last in her physical presence. I remember vividly some of her last words to me. She held my hand, looked me straight in the eye, and lovingly said "I will be leaving you soon, and when you think of me always think of love." My response, "is there anything else I would think of?" Thank you grandma, you will be forever in my heart and on my mind. *Teen Wise* was scheduled to be released exactly six years later, on March 26th, 2009, to honor her legacy of love. However, circumstances beyond my control detained its release for nearly one month.

To my one and only child whom I completely adore and cherish. Parenting you has guided me to discover a new found strength that continuously inspired me to finish this book and find my real purpose in life. I thank you for the opportunity to experience our exceptional relationship.

A special acknowledgment goes to my Uncle Bob Gonsalves and Aunty Bev Gonsalves for the love and support I have received from them over the years. I thank you from the bottom of my heart for investing your time in listening to me and always allowing me to "be me." Your encouragement and commitment to provide me with unconditional love has surpassed and superseded all my expectations. I thank you dearly.

For my "guy" friends that I refer to as my artificial brothers: Christopher Summo, John Jerves, and Douglas Leandro. I really appreciate your belief in this project and the special, personal attention you've all given me over the years. I wish you only the absolute best and always remember your daughters will always hold a special place in my heart. I thank you profoundly and profusely.

1

As for my girlfriends, through the last few years I have had many enter and exit my life for various reasons. The one friend that has exhibited an exemplary, healthy friendship pattern for many years is Marilyn Patton. Your commitment to our relationship, unwavering support, and genuine belief in me is a true testament to the wonderful person you are. I am a better person for knowing you. I thank you wholeheartedly.

Most of all, I thank you, the reader, for choosing *Teen Wise* as a guide for preteens and teenagers. Whether you are a preteen or a teenager, a concerned parent of a preteen or a teenager, a person who works closely with preteens and/or teenagers, or a person who has the best interest of preteens and teenagers at heart, I sincerely hope you find this book purposeful and beneficial. My extended appreciation goes out to all of you.

Introduction

My intention for writing this book is to offer a communicative venue for teenagers, parents, teachers, counselors, and any concerned citizen that has a teenager's best interest at heart. Its purpose is to support the natural interaction progress between teenager and adult, thus bridging the gap. Guiding teenagers to acquire the power of self-definition by adapting the concept of Self-Serving Strategies for the betterment of their future is the main goal of this book. Self-Serving Strategies allow an individual to analyze a situation or dilemma to come up with the best possible solution that may benefit his/her future, without infringing on another person's rights or intentionally hurting someone in the process. Learning how to acquire the power of self-definition may prepare a teenager to make decisions that best define who they are now and the person they want to become in the future, by making choices in their best self-interest. Taking responsibility for one's own actions, beliefs, consequences, and directional path may enable a teenager to refocus by internalizing his/her prospective future. Emphasis is strictly on the self.

This book contains ten chapters for the reader to explore and grasp the concept presented. Chapter one is labeled the "Wise Segments," that are categorized by title, which include "Addiction Wise," "Friendship Wise," "Dating Wise," "Romantic Relationship Wise," and "Parent Wise." Each segment is composed of information pertaining to the specific subject matter in the form of advice, experiences, and opinions and/or views that are solely and completely from my own perspective. Chapters two through eight are labeled by grade level, beginning with the sixth grade and ending with the twelfth. These chapters encourage cognitive reasoning and decision making skills by providing ten different situational scenarios, along with three different answer choices and a possible result for each example presented. An explanation of a possible result is described as either a consequence or a benefit that may occur based on the option chosen. There are a few examples that list a consequence and a benefit as possible results for that chosen option because of the complex subject matter. The examples illustrated are truly fictitious; however, it is probable for a teenager to encounter one or more of these instances in his/her own daily life. Each individual's circumstance is unique to his/her own environment and/or experiences; therefore, an outcome is nearly impossible to predict. The consequence or benefit given represents an opportunity to examine his/her foreseeable future from a different motivational factor. It is not intended to signify a guarantee. The federal government mandates Chapter 19 rules and regulations for all public schools in the United States. You can receive a copy from your local public school for review. A few examples have Chapter 19 references of certain violations such as truancy, harassment, and plagiarism, which are presented as part of a consequence for that specific answer choice. It is intended for the teenager to realize the severity of violating these rules. Chapter nine consists of Six Bonus Fundamentals essential to live efficiently by enabling a person to perform at optimum production levels. Chapter ten completes this publication with a reiteration of the concept introduced and a special message from me, Ms. Celeste.

My main goal is to play an instrumental role in the implementation of Self-Serving Strategies in the young minds of today's teenagers; with the hope of fostering this concept into their everyday lives for the betterment of their future. I am honored you have chosen to read this book. Please use the information offered as a guide to practicing this concept with a goal of retaining as much knowledge as possible for future reference.

Thank you very much for your valuable time, Ms. Celeste.

Chapter #1
The Wise Segments

This first chapter of *Teen Wise* is composed of different "Wise" segments that provide information pertaining to the subject matter in the form of advice, experience, opinions, and/or views that are solely and completely from my own perspective. The following "Wise" segments introduced and included in this chapter are "Addiction Wise," "Friendship Wise," "Dating Wise," "Romantic Relationship Wise," and "Parent Wise." Please review the segments for comprehension and consider using and/or referring to the advice when contemplating any of the five subject matters presented.

Addiction Wise

When faced with a decision to smoke a cigarette, drink an alcoholic beverage, or intake any type of illegal drug, you really do not know how you are going to react. You may not have the control you once owned. All it may take is once. In your family tree, you may already carry a predisposed gene to addictive diseases; however, if there is no known history of any addiction in your family of origin, you could be the sprout of a new tree that starts this genetic predisposing for generations to inherit. So, you really don't know what you will lose if you take that first puff, sip, or swallow. You will almost always give up something for any of these choices.

A person may become an addict from curiosity. Wanting to know what it would feel like to become intoxicated or high is the type of curiosity that need not be exercised. Instead, a healthier suggestion to curb your curious nature would be to wonder what it would feel like if you were to win a championship game in your chosen sport, or to be acknowledged for academic achievement, or to become class president, or to be known as a positive influence by young, impressionable children, or to be appreciated for your active contribution to your community. You can custom tailor your inquisitiveness to meet your own talents, needs, and wants. Let creativity be your inspiration. Take that first step by taking a step back to reanalyze your position and to modify your purpose, then proceed.

If you are currently or have taken any of these harmful substances to help numb you from any type of abuse or emotional heartbreak, learning how to develop healthy solutions to pain may prove to be a life changing alternative. Suggestions include, but are not limited to, talking to an adult you can trust, seeking counsel from a reputable psychologist or equivalent counselor, and implementing a new plan of action when the urge to engage in disruptive behavior occurs. A new plan of action could be as simple as exercising or devoting your spare time to something that you are truly passionate about. The goal is to develop healthy coping skills by keeping your mind occupied with things that you enjoy doing; however, healing from the original source of your pain is the key to living a healthy and productive lifestyle. Therefore, I strongly encourage you to enter a therapy regimen that focuses on an approach that fosters this goal.

Interestingly, Mr. Donald Trump, real estate developer and multi-billionaire, has never smoked a cigarette, drunk an alcoholic beverage, or consumed any illegal drug. He has publicly vowed to never engage in any such activity in his lifetime. By making this conscience choice he was able to discover his true potential. His decision has enabled him to perform at his optimal health level on a daily basis, free from the possibility of developing diseases and illnesses that cigarette smoking may bring on, free from dealing with the sluggish, painful feeling a hang-over may bring on, and free from the adverse effects illegal drugs may bring on. This proves that a healthy body with a clear mind can definitely produce successful results. The measurement of your own success rate is a valuable resource for you to attain.

Friendship Wise

When establishing a friendship base, strive for the best because that is what you deserve. You are responsible for the realm you decide to place yourself in. The people you associate with are a direct reflection of who you are and the way others will perceive you. For example, if you hang-out with a group that engages in drug activities, but you do not participate, people will assume you are just by association, which will produce a false impression of you. Observation of character traits, morals, and beliefs, along with finding a few things in common, is a good place to begin. A great friend is one who exhibits a reciprocal friendship pattern. For instance, one who returns your phone calls and favors in a timely manner is classified as a give and take relationship. Great qualities a good friend will display are: Respect for you and your belongings, keeping your secrets, will not speak negatively or gossip about you to others, practices open communication, will not make everything about him/her, and is trustworthy. An unhealthy friendship, one that breaches any of the previous examples, needs to be addressed because you do not need to tolerate anyone who is treating you with less than what you deserve. Dissolving a friendship is never an easy task to undertake; however, by practicing Self-Serving Strategies you may come to realize some of the best decisions that you may need to make on your own behalf may be the most difficult. Putting yourself and your future first will benefit you in all aspects of your life. Take a look around you right now and start to evaluate your choices in friends. Eliminate any unwanted friends, if necessary and begin to foster and nurture the positive, healthy ones. A really good friendship has the potential to last a lifetime.

Dating Wise

The purpose of dating is to get to know another individual with the hopes of finding that special person that shares common interests and hobbies with you. It is perfectly acceptable to date more than one person at a time; however, discussing your intentions with the people involved may help to eliminate any undue heartache and/or expectations. Communication is the key to successful dating. An example of a real date is one that allows two people to be alone, for a specified amount of time if chaperoned, to engage in an activity. Deciding who will take on the monetary responsibility of the outing beforehand may prevent an awkward moment from happening at any time during the date. Shared responsibility, not dutch or halves, is a good balance because it takes the pressure off. Shared, meaning one person may volunteer to pay for the meal, while the other flips for the movie and popcorn. Dutch, meaning both people pay for only what he/she has ordered, which may make either person feel uncomfortable. Halves mean that everything is split fifty-fifty across the board, which I don't recommend because the focus of the date may be tainted by visionary division playing out in your mind. A small gift given by either person is a kind gesture to set the tone of the date. Small gift, meaning a simple card or a single rose for him/her. Yes, it's okay to give a guy a rose or two. I have done it on more than one occasion and they were all pleasantly surprised. Enjoy the person you have chosen to spend your valuable time with. Dating is a process that takes time, energy, and practice, so take things slowly. You may not want to believe this, but time is on your side. Please remember, the purpose is to get to know someone for whom he/she is; therefore, there is no obligatory condition a person must fulfill just because he/she has agreed to go out with you. Happy dating!

Romantic Relationship Wise

When you have been dating someone for a while, don't assume that you are entitled to refer to him/her as your boyfriend/girlfriend without a discussion. This title represents a commitment that requires conversational communication between both people. By having this "talk," you and the other person will know exactly where he/she stands in the development of your relationship. This agreement also allows each person certain rights and responsibilities. For example, as a boyfriend/girlfriend you have the right to bring any inappropriate behavior to his/her attention. Dating does not give you just cause to question him/her. Caring and loving another human being in itself is a responsibility that involves attention, dedication, and energy.

There are two kinds of romantic relationships you need to be aware of, healthy and unhealthy. Observation and knowing the person you've become are key factors in developing healthy, romantic relationships. A healthy relationship is one that exhibits respect and support for each other's goals and vision for the future, a level of understanding if plans don't include him/her, a genuine love for each other, and no abuse pattern. An unhealthy relationship is one that displays abusive components that include, but are not limited to, disrespectful mannerisms, interpersonal violence, directional profanity (lazy language), reactionary yelling, possessive traits, and sexual misconduct.

If you are currently involved in an unhealthy relationship, examining yourself from the inside out may help to clarify why you have chosen this person in your life. Start by looking deep within yourself to explore any experiences that may have attributed to your tolerance level. At some point you may have been taught by example that it is okay to be treated this way. Well, it is never okay to be treated with any abusive component. Never. You are worth it. Keep telling yourself over and over again, in a mirror if it is more effective for you, "I am worth it!" Receptive counseling may help you gain the knowledge of the cycle of abuse and relationship dynamics that may enable you to establish healthier relationships in the future. However, change is a process that entails time and a real commitment of disclosure to reach a successful outcome. You may seek the advice from your school counselor or family doctor for a referral. Here's something to think about: If you begin your journey to self-discovery today, you would have taken the first step for better tomorrows.

Parent Wise

A great alternative to punishment is the opportunity to implement a teaching element. A lesson learned, from your child's eyes is a

9

valuable asset that may help to prevent future temptations and implications. One of our jobs as parents is to prepare our children for the real world; however, this task is not an easy one to master.

The following suggestions should be used at your discretion and, whenever possible, try to directly relate the lesson to the actual offense. Personally, I have either done or will do, if the need arises, some of these examples. I have had positive results for the few that I have enforced.

Example #1: If you are being challenged by instilling a respect element as a character trait in your child, you may want to require him/her to complete a series of "good deeds" in your community. A rule of thumb is that the person receiving the kind gesture cannot be familiar or related to the giver.

> A few suggestions of "good deeds" are as follows:
> a) Standing in front of a grocery store and offering people help with their grocery bags.
> b) Help younger children cross the street.
> c) Read books to young children at your local library.
> d) Volunteer at any charitable organization.

Any suggestion can be modified to suit your needs and goals. It is important for you, as the parent, to let your child take on the responsibility of contacting the sources to complete his/her obligations. All you need to provide him/her with is a specified number of "good deeds" to be fulfilled by a reasonable deadline. Please take age and maturity level into consideration. An enormous quantity is not necessary to produce a positive result. Administer accordingly.

You may witness, over time, a shift in your child's appreciation and expectation levels; thus instilling a respect element.

Example #2: If you gave your child permission to borrow an item that belongs to you, for example your bike, and he/she loses it, breaks it, or it gets stolen while in his/her possession, then it is his/her responsibility to replace the item.

A suggestion to remedy this situation would be to allow your child ample time to EARN the money to purchase a new or used item comparable to the one you once owned. For this lesson to be effective the money that is needed to replace your item shouldn't come from your child's savings account or monetary birthday gifts. Earned monies may come from doing extra chores around the house, odd jobs around the neighborhood, or an after school job (age permitting).

Your child may think twice about borrowing something from you, or anyone, because he/she will have learned how much responsibility is entailed to ensure the return of that item, if something goes wrong; thus instilling a responsibility element.

Example #3: If your unlicensed child decides to steal the family car and go joy riding with his/her friends and gets home safely, then he/she needs to be taught a reality element. Most teenagers have an invincible mindset, the belief system that nothing bad will ever happen to them. The severity of his/her choice and the irreversible consequences that may have followed this decision needs to be acknowledged by him/her.

> A few suggestions to instill a reality element are as follows:
> a) Take him/her to a funeral or gravesite of a young person who died from making a decision involving an automobile (car racing, drunk driving, and/or being unlicensed) that proved to be detrimental to his/her life.
> b) Require an essay to be written by him/her that consists of current statistics and data pertaining to the adverse affects that have occurred from irresponsible teenage

driving in your community or state. Include research on an individual's personal story.

c) Require him/her to pay a portion of the car insurance bill from EARNED monies.

You may use any suggestion stated above in any combination, or you may want to invent your own reality lesson. Hopefully, the realization of the seriousness of his/her actions will be acknowledged by your child before it's too late; thus instilling a reality element.

Chapter #2
The Sixth Grade

I decided to incorporate the sixth grade into *Teen Wise* to give you a preview of the many challenges that you may soon encounter. Becoming familiar with the concept of Self-Serving Strategies at the onset of your preteen years may enable you to be more effective, as practice equals experience.

There are ten scenarios that depict dilemmas and character building opportunities. After each explanation three different choices follow, along with the probability of a consequence or a benefit for that specific decision, which may occur. In examples #5-C and #10-C there is a consequence and a benefit listed as possible results due to the actions presented in the answer choices. To provide a broad spectrum of examples, some relate to a student that is enrolled in the sixth grade at an elementary school, some at a middle/intermediate school, and some are written in general.

#1.) You are in the sixth grade and you just purchased some merchandise at your local drug store. The cashier gives you your change and you notice that he/she has given you five dollars too much. The cashier has gone on to his/her next transaction, without realizing his/her mistake. You know that taking this money would be dishonest; however, you think that since the cashier didn't recognize his/her mistake it would be okay. What are your options?

A.) You decide to leave the store without letting the cashier know. You fully understand that the cashier will have to take responsibility by replacing the five dollars in his/her cash box at the end of his/her shift. You don't feel bad because he/she should know how to do his/her job correctly. You are ashamed of your decision, so you don't share this experience with anyone.
Consequence: You will always know in the back of your head that you did not do the right thing, thus creating a negative memory for yourself. Because this money did not belong to you in the first

place, this action is considered stealing. You may think that you got away with it, but this behavior may lead you down the wrong path. This is not an example of using Self-Serving Strategies because your choice was dishonest, which may affect your future in a negative manner.

B.) You decide to leave the store and tell all your neighborhood friends how you scored five extra dollars. You continue to brag the next day in school. Your friends think it's cool, but your sister doesn't and decides to tell your parents. You apologize and get in trouble for your dishonesty.

Consequence: Because you apologized for getting caught and not the behavior itself, you did not learn anything. Taking money that is not yours is considered stealing. Your parents may become less trusting of you, which could cause a communication break-down in the near future. This is not an example of using Self-Serving Strategies because you not only took the money, you also bragged about it. These behaviors, if continued, may affect your future negatively.

C.) You bring it to the attention of the cashier immediately after you realize his/her mistake. The cashier double checks your receipt and confirms the oversight. You return the money. He/she thanks you for being a model citizen.

Benefit: You feel good about yourself because you did the right thing. You realize that in the long run you did what was best for you because you don't have to carry the weight of a negative choice. There is only a positive memory from this experience. You begin to gain a sense of who you are. You start to build admirable character and trust beneficial to your future. Congratulations on practicing Self Serving Strategies effectively and acquiring the power of self-definition.

#2.) You are in the sixth grade and attend a middle/intermediate school. You have had the same best friend since kindergarten. You begin to notice a change in your friend's behavior with you. For example, he/she hasn't returned your phone calls and has avoided you in school for the past few days. The next day in school, your friend approaches you and offers you a drag of a cigarette. You are shocked that your friend has taken up smoking, but not surprised because you knew something was up. You want to keep your friendship with him/her, but don't know if it is a good idea since he/she is now smoking. What are your options?

A.) You really don't want to smoke; however, you decide to try it because you don't want to lose your friend or cause yourself any embarrassment. After all, one drag will not make you a smoker and you get to keep your friend.

Consequence: You didn't stay true to yourself by putting your own needs first. You displayed characteristics of becoming a follower, which may have a negative impact on your future. This choice may lead you to become addicted to tobacco in the near future. Please refer to "Addiction Wise" and "Friendship Wise" in Chapter #1: The Wise Segments for a recap. This is not an example of using Self-Serving Strategies because you compromised yourself and you may become addicted to cigarette smoking, which may affect your future and health negatively.

B.) You turn your friend's offer down. Your friend gets mad and calls you a baby for not wanting to smoke, then walks away from you. You are hurt because you knew this person since you were five years old, but you know that smoking is not a cool thing to do. You terminate this friendship because it has become unhealthy for you.

Benefit: You stayed true to yourself by making decisions that best suited your needs. You demonstrated leadership qualities that may enable you to make wise choices in the near future. Although you are hurt from the dissolution of your friendship, you realize that a real friend wouldn't have treated you in a disrespectful manner, as described in "Friendship Wise" in Chapter #1: The Wise Segments. You become proud of yourself for not giving in to peer pressure in this situation. Congratulations on a great example of using Self-Serving Strategies proficiently and acquiring the power of self-definition.

15

C.) You react with anger. Even though you want to keep your friendship, you become overwhelmed with anger and decide to confront your friend. You tell him/her that smoking is not cool. You give him/her an ultimatum between your friendship, which includes not smoking and dropping his/her "new" friends.

Consequence: This action you chose to take may be the start of a pattern of trying to fix people. This is not an example of being a supportive friend. The only person you are responsible for is yourself. You may be empowering your friend by giving him/her the option to remain friends. Also, this person may resent you for your actions. Learning the concept of Self-Serving Strategies may train you to respond to a situation like this by having your best self-interest in mind. Doing what is right for you. This is not an example of using Self-Serving Strategies because you reacted with anger and tried to fix your friend's problem.

#3.) You are in the sixth grade and attend an elementary school. You and your classmates are walking to the cafeteria for lunch. A few of your classmates begin to tease the first graders who are on the field playing during recess. You are shocked at their behavior and aren't sure what to do. You know that telling your teacher may cause you to be labeled a "tattletale," but you know it is wrong to tease anyone (especially younger children). What are your options?

A.) You decide to reconcile the feelings of these first graders by actively connecting with them. You volunteer to read and have frequent chats with this group. You understand the importance of being a role model for the lower grade levels. You encourage their self-esteem growth by building their tolerance level. You teach them that it is never okay to tease someone, even if it was done to you first. You were not concerned of any teasing that may have come your way because you decided to help these first graders.

Benefit: Your decision not only benefited these first graders, but it also benefited you. You achieved your goal of providing them a positive role model to look-up to. You exhibited impeccable leadership skills that may enable you to build a foundation for your future endeavors. You can leave this school when you graduate, with confidence in knowing that you were responsible for making a difference in these young children's lives. Congratulations on a wonderful example of Self-Serving Strategies effectively and acquiring the power of self-definition.

B.) You make the conscious choice to play along with this group because you don't want them to tease you if you don't. You know that it is wrong to hurt anyone's feelings. You begin to feel awful about your decision and hope that your actions will not produce any long term, negative affects for any of these children.

Consequence: You may think that you did what was best for you by preventing anyone to tease you, but your decision may have caused hurtful feelings for these first graders. Thus, NOT practicing Self-Serving Strategies! The definition is located in the introduction for a recap. You may have caused yourself to experience undue stress, worry, and disappointment for going along with something that you knew in your heart was wrong; therefore not staying true to yourself. You gave into peer pressure at the expense of innocent children. You also demonstrated characteristics of becoming a follower, which may be detrimental to your future plans and goals. Please rethink your choices, and refocus your purpose.

C.) You confront this group of classmates and tell them to stop! An argument breaks out between you and them. Their position in the fight is that you should mind your own business and yours is to speak-up for the innocent first graders being teased. The commotion has drawn the attention of the teacher and you all get sent to the office to speak to the vice-principal.

Consequence: You may think that by advocating for the younger students, you were doing the right thing. Unfortunately, that was not the outcome. Your decision put you in a confrontational position with these classmates, who have already proven their lack of respect for others. You may be reprimanded for the argument that followed your statement, which may remain on your school record. Although your intentions were to protect the children, learning when and with whom to voice your convictions may help to eliminate any backlash you might face in the future. This is not an example of using Self-Serving Strategies correctly.

#4.) You are in the sixth grade and walking home from school with some friends. It is 2:15 p.m. and you need to be home by 3:00 p.m. Your friends have plans to go to the nearby bowling alley to play video games and want you to join them. You know that if you go, you will not be home on time. You want to go, but don't want to jeopardize the special plans you have for the upcoming weekend. What are your options?

A.) You decide to call home and ask for permission to go. Your mom gives you the okay and tells you to be home no later than 4:30 pm. You go with your friends, have a great time, and get home by 4:30 p.m.
Benefit: You have learned that it doesn't hurt to ask when you want something. You displayed leadership when asking your mom for what you wanted. You showed her that you can be trusted and responsible, which may result in more freedom for you in the near future. You are able to go ahead with the special plans you have for the upcoming weekend. This is a great example of practicing Self-Serving Strategies. Congratulations!

B.) You decide to go without permission and you have a great time. Before you know it, the time has passed and you realize that it is now 5:00 p.m.! You rush home and make it there in fifteen minutes. You notice a lot of people at your house and begin to wonder what happened. Well, being that this was the first time you have ever not come home on time, your mom had called a few people in the neighborhood to help look for you. You were nearly two and a half hours late, with no phone call! Your mom was worried and thought something had happened to you. After all the excitement calmed down, you get grounded for the next two weeks, which means your plans for the upcoming weekend are off! You apologize to your mother.
Consequence: You showed characteristics of becoming a follower when you agreed to go with your friends without permission,

although you knew it was wrong. You caused your mom to worry unnecessarily. It may take a while for you to gain her trust back. You may think you benefited from your choice because you had a lot of fun, but this is not an example of practicing Self-Serving Strategies because your actions caused undue hurt and worry for someone else. The definition is located in the Introduction for a recap.

C.) You decide to tell your friends you can't go because you have to be home by 3:00 p.m. You go home and get your homework and chores done. Your plans for the weekend are not jeopardized.
Benefit: You stayed true to yourself by doing what was right, following the rules. This is an example of practicing Self-Serving Strategies because you did what was best for you, without hurting anyone in the process. This decision also guaranteed your plans for the upcoming weekend wouldn't be jeopardized. Playing it safe is admirable, but next time you may want to try asking your mom if you can go, after all, it doesn't hurt to ask. You did not give into temptations, which is an instinct that you have learned to control in this situation. Being able to trust yourself is an invaluable trait to have. Congratulations!

#5.) You are in the sixth grade and a classmate has asked you if he/she could cheat off your test paper in class today. This person is very popular in school and letting him/her cheat may put you in the "in" crowd. The test is scheduled after lunch recess, which gives you all morning to ponder a decision. You want to be considered popular too, but you know that cheating is very wrong. What are your options?

A.) You decide to make a deal to let him/her cheat, and he/she agrees to become your friend and includes you with the popular crowd. You both cheat on the test, but the teacher catches you. Your classmate acts innocent, however you are both sent to the office to be reprimanded. Your classmate continues to pretend to not know what is going on. The vice-principal interviews both of you separately and gets two different stories. You each receive

19

detention after school for two weeks, a zero for the test, and a parent notification letter that needs to be signed and returned the next day of school. The original deal has been revoked because you were unable to successfully allow him/her to cheat.

Consequence: Your choice may have caused your after school activities to be interrupted. For example, if you play team sports you may not be able to attend your mandatory practices, which may prevent you from playing in any upcoming games. Belonging to a sports team requires commitment and responsibility; therefore, you may let your teammates down. Your focus in this decision was to be included with your popular peers, at whatever the cost. You may have compromised your values and yourself for the sake of peer pressure of being seen with the "in" crowd. This was clearly not acting in your own best self-interest; therefore, it is not an example of using Self-Serving Strategies. This reprimand may remain on your school record, which may disqualify you from the consideration of awards and/or recommendations in your near future. *Please Note: Your value comes from who you are as a person and not from the people you are seen with.

B.) You decide to tell your classmate the answer is "No!" He/ she went on to ask another classmate for the same favor and the person agreed to the terms. You witnessed them cheating during the test, but the teacher didn't recognize what was going on. The next day in school you see them together hanging out with the popular crowd. You just go on about your own daily business and don't let it bother you.

Benefit: You stayed true to yourself by knowing and doing what was right for you. Not willing to take a chance on cheating proves that you are thinking of the consequences that may result from such an action beforehand. This is a sign of growing-up and taking responsibility for yourself. You realize that just because they got away with cheating on this day, their future still may be affected. You have come to the understanding that behavior like this can lead to riskier decisions that may have adverse outcomes. You definitely displayed Self-Serving Strategies and acquired the power of self-definition. Congratulations!

C.) You go along with the original plan and are able to successfully cheat. Your classmate begins to include you with his/her crowd. You discover, over a course of a few days, that this popular group engages in intimidation tactics against students they feel are not good enough to be in their presence. You do not agree with their actions, but you are now recognized as being associated with them. You slowly realized that being involved with this group was not worth the dishonesty you had to portray to be admitted. You distance yourself from them and reconnect with your "real" friends.

Consequence: Because you know it is wrong to cheat, but you still made the decision to do so, you did not stay true to yourself or practice Self-Serving Strategies. Not getting caught for cheating is irrelevant in this situation because the focus is on the choice you made and not the outcome itself.

Benefit: Because you observed the actions of this group over the course of a few days and quickly determined that you did not want to be associated with them, you then displayed Self-Serving Strategies. You can recognize the fact that you initially made the wrong choice, but after observing their inappropriate behavior, you took the proper steps to disconnect your association with this popular group; however, by practicing Self-Serving Strategies at the onset of a situation, you will be able to help alleviate any undue stress and negative experiences that a wrong decision may bring on as a result.

#6.) You are in the sixth grade and have decided to enter a contest, where the winners are determined by student votes, at your school. Unbeknownst to you, one of your closest friends has entered the same contest. Your friend talks about it all the time, with certainty that he/she will win. The results of the voting ballets reveal that YOU are indeed the winner. You have won the first place position, while your friend took second. Your friend becomes very upset with you and begins to display jealous behavior. You are proud of yourself for placing first in the contest, but don't know how to deal with your friends feelings. What are your options?

A.) You decide to forfeit your winning position because you realize how important this contest is to your friend. He/she now has the chance to take-over your first place position. Your intention was to be a good friend by recognizing the disappointment your friend was experiencing and doing something to help alleviate his/her pain.

Consequence: Although you think that your decision would be classified as "being a good friend," it doesn't. You are not responsible for fixing your friend's experience by sacrificing something that you earned. You did not stay true to yourself. This contest was conducted fairly; therefore, you couldn't control the outcome. This is not an example of using Self-Serving Strategies.

B.) You decide to confront your friend about his/her behavior and you begin arguing. You try to explain to him/her that the students' votes were calculated and the results were that you were the first place winner and he/she came in second. The argument escalates into a fist fight on school campus, you both get suspended for the next two days, and you are both stripped of your winning positions.

Consequence: You jeopardized an opportunity for yourself by choosing to confront an already angry friend, when he/she was clearly not ready to communicate. This decision has earned you a suspension record and the disqualification of being a contest winner. This is not an example of developing good leadership skills, or using Self-Serving Strategies.

C.) You decide to let your friend vent all he/she wants to. You tell him/her that you will be there for support, if the need arose. You accept your first place position with pride.

Benefit: You stayed true to yourself and remained a good friend by accepting the honor graciously and offering support at the same time. Congratulations! This is an example of exercising Self-Serving Strategies proficiently.

#7.) You are in the sixth grade and attend a middle/intermediate school. You have been approached by an eighth grader to complete a dare. The dare is to pull the fire alarm in school during an important test the eighth graders need to take the next day. This action will cause a false alarm and the fire department will be notified. The person has told you that if you do not successfully execute the dare he/she will tell the whole school that you are a "chicken." You know that it is wrong, but you are afraid of being teased by the whole school. What are your options?

A.) You decide to pull the fire alarm and the fire department arrives at your school to investigate the situation. After a careful assessment, the fire chief discovered the alarm was pulled as a prank. Time, money, and manpower were wasted. Later that evening, the news reported a REAL fire five blocks from your school that started approximately twenty minutes after you pulled the alarm at your school. The fire department was unable to reach this house in a timely manner because it was investigating the school prank that you did. When the fire trucks finally arrived, the house and its contents were destroyed. People were taken to the nearby hospital, with no word on their condition.

Consequence: This choice may have taken the lives of people who were really in need of the fire department's services. Just because the school did not realize that you are responsible for this terrible crime, does not necessarily mean that you got away with it. You will always have the memory of being responsible for other people's misfortune and hardship by playing the dare game. Loss of property can be replaced, but life is a precious blessing that is irreplaceable. This is not an example of practicing Self-Serving Strategies by the avoidance of being teased because your decision had caused you to commit a crime that, as a result, hurt innocent people in the process. You knew it was wrong, but you went ahead any way. This is an example of becoming a follower. By learning and practicing Self-Serving Strategies you may, over time, acquire leadership skills that may directly impact your future in a positive manner.

B.) You decide to pull the fire alarm and the fire department arrived at your school to investigate the situation. After a careful assessment, the fire chief discovered that the alarm was pulled as a prank. Time, money, and manpower were wasted. A few days went by, and the results of the fingerprint analysis were in. The

Principal made one last effort to give the culprit or culprit's a chance to come forward to take responsibility for his/her actions during an announcement over a school wide speaker system. You still did not step-up to claim responsibility. You did not know that finger-prints were taken. The next day the Principal called you in to his/her office where your parents were waiting for you. Because of the severity of your crime, expulsion was determined as the right course of discipline. The State's school district has a zero tolerance law for crimes that may affect loss of life and/or property, which is defined as a Chapter 19 violation. By occupying the fire department for a false alarm, you could have prevented a REAL fire from being tended to in a timely manner.

Consequence: Because you were expelled from school, your parents will need to find another school that will accept you in your district. Your expulsion documentation will remain on your school record until you enter high school. This is an example of becoming a follower. By learning and practicing Self-Serving Strategies you will, over time, acquire leadership skills that may directly impact your future in a positive manner.

C.) You decide to tell this eighth grader that you are not interested in executing this dare and walk away. Students called you a "chicken" the next day in school, but you did not let it bother you because you fully understood how dangerous this prank may have been if it was carried out. Since the information circulated through-out the school, it was near impossible for this eighth grader to find someone else to do his deceptive work in time. The fire alarm was never pulled under false pretenses.

Benefit: You stayed true to yourself by knowing that you could handle a little teasing. You displayed admirable leadership skills by doing what was right, despite the uncomfortable backlash you faced by other students. You have empowered yourself by being able to walk away from a possible dangerous situation that could have proven deadly for innocent people. Peer pressure did not influence your decision, maturity did. Congratulations! This is a wonderful example of practicing Self-Serving Strategies. You also acquired the power of self-definition.

#8.) You are in the sixth grade and attend an elementary school. You have earned the respect from your teachers by achieving a high grade point average and by exhibiting polite mannerisms with classmates and other faculty members. You have been recommended to become a mentor to a few third graders at your school. The requirements entail you to conduct supportive meetings with them during lunch recess twice a week for eight consecutive weeks. You are very interested and consider it an honor to be recognized for the position; however, a few of your friends, that weren't asked to participate in the program, have begun to tease you about becoming a role model. These so called friends are trying to convince you that you are not qualified and you begin to doubt your own abilities. You want to pursue this opportunity because you believe it would be an asset on your school record and you want to gain experience, but you don't want your friends to continue teasing you for the entire eight weeks. What are your options?

A.) You decide to accept the offer of becoming a mentor to a few third graders because you realize that your friends are probably reacting out of jealously and not factual evidence of your inability to fulfill the mentoring role. You know that if they were your real friends, as defined in "Friendship Wise" in Chapter #1: The Wise Segments, they would not be treating you disrespectfully. You also decide to reexamine your choice in these friendships from a different perspective to determine if the relationships are healthy for you.

Benefit: You stayed true to yourself by making a decision in your best self-interest, despite any ramifications others may try to place on you. Your confidence level may have been boosted by the commitment you made to invest your time and knowledge by mentoring these third graders. Upon completion of the program, you may receive recognition and/or an award for your accomplishment, documented on your transcript.

Congratulations, this is a clear example of exercising Self-Serving Strategies effectively.

B.) You decide to mentor these third graders secretly because you don't want to deal with any teasing that may occur if your decision is publicly known.

Consequence: By hiding your volunteer efforts, you may have taught these third graders that you are ashamed of helping them. You did not display confidence in yourself by keeping the meetings and events private. Since you attend a small school, your friends eventually find out what you are doing and they tease you even more. Please refer to "Friendship Wise" in Chapter #1: The Wise Segments to help you determine if these relationships are healthy for you. You are providing a service for your school and community, which may have been celebrated and recognized; however, by hiding, you may not be acknowledged for the difference you've made in the lives of these young eight and nine year olds. This is not an example of practicing Self-Serving Strategies because you may have hurt yourself in the process by not exuding confidence and you may have hurt others by instilling shame. Doing the right thing is great, but not when your decision involves deception to avoid any backlash you may face for it. No one wins!

C.) You turn the offer down because you just don't think you are good enough to help third graders. Your friends have convinced you that you would be wasting your time because you don't have any knowledge to contribute.

Consequence: You did not exhibit any confidence in yourself to believe that you have the skills needed for this mentoring position. You did not evaluate the facts in this matter. First of all, your teachers recognized your abilities by observing your character traits, polite manners, and academic standing. It is an honor to be recommended for a mentoring position because the recognition means that they are entrusting you with young, impressionable minds. Please review "Friendship Wise" in Chapter #1: The Wise Segments, to determine if these people you consider your friends truly represent the definition and examples given. You may want to do a self-evaluation assessment of yourself to analyze why you were so easily convinced of your inability to take on this task. Sometimes fear and self-doubt over shadow a decision, but using an excuse because it's easier than disclosing the truth may prove to be counter-productive. Everyone experiences fear, especially when faced with a new opportunity. This is not an example of using Self-Serving Strategies because you forfeited an opportunity for yourself that may have benefited your future positively.

#9.) You are in the sixth grade and attend a middle/intermediate school. The school bell has just rung to begin homeroom and everyone is rushing to their classes. You drop your books on the floor and bend down to pick them up. As you reach for it, your pants rips in the back and your under clothes are revealed. A few classmates witness your embarrassing moment and begin to laugh out loud. You don't like being made fun of and are not sure of how to handle it. What are your options?

A.) You decide to ask your teacher for a pass to go to the health room because you are so embarrassed. There you call your parents to come pick you up. You convince them that you can't go back to school that day and they grant you with a "free" day. The next morning you pretend to be sick, but this time your parents don't give in. You return to school and you soon realize that a lot of people know about yesterday's incident. They laugh and call you names. You had to relive that moment the entire school day. Eventually, your story became old news and those people found someone new to tease.

Consequence: By running from this embarrassing situation you may have created more attention for yourself. Your actions allowed your fellow classmates time to think about the incident because you did not deal with it in that moment. This decision also may have caused you to experience undue stress and anxiety, since you tried to skip school the next day because you still did not want to face it. Although teasing and name calling are hurtful, realizing that you didn't consider these classmates to be your friends from the beginning may have helped to reduce your anxiousness. Considering the source of any infliction, combined with knowing who you really are, may give you better insight in handling another situation similar to this one. People experience unforeseen embarrassing moments all the time, but their survival and recovery depends upon which way they choose to react and deal with it. Laugh at yourself and others will laugh with you, not at you. For all these reasons, this is not an example of using Self-Serving Strategies.

B.) You decide to laugh with them. You think quickly to grab your jacket and tie it around your waist. The laughing begins to subside. You go on with the school day as if nothing ever happened.

Benefit: By instilling humor in a very embarrassing situation you were able to alleviate the teasing. This reaction may have been surprising to the people who were laughing at you; therefore, they had no other choice, but to stop because there was no longer a payoff. Their mission to get to you did not work. By having the ability to laugh at yourself, you displayed confidence in knowing who you are. You did what was best for you without hurting anyone in the process, thus practicing Self-Serving Strategies.

C.) You decide to react with anger and start yelling at the classmates that are laughing and teasing you. The screaming and yelling escalates into a fight with the person that seems to be the leader responsible for your humiliation. A teacher breaks-up the fight and sends you both to the office to seek counsel with the vice principal. There is a zero tolerance law in your state for violence that all public schools must abide by; therefore, the police were called. Since you both hit each other, you both get arrested. You are later picked-up at the police station by your parents. You both get suspended from school for three days.

Consequence: You used anger to try to defuse an embarrassing situation, which did not work. Instead you created an extremely hostile environment for you and your classmates to endure. Witnessing violence can be just as damaging as being a participant of it. Your reaction and behavioral choice resulted in an arrest, a suspension, and a disciplinary school record. You may also receive other punishments from your parents. This decision was definitely not made with your best self-interest in mind; therefore, it is not an example of using Self-Serving Strategies.

#10.) You are in the sixth grade and attend an elementary school. You are very excited to play sports on a competitive team and you tried your very best at try-outs to show your athletic abilities; however, you don't have any prior experience in playing organized sports. The coach posted the team line-up the next day and you soon realize that your name is not on the roster. You really want to play on this team and are very upset that you did not make it. What are your options?

A.) You request a meeting with the coach to discuss the main reasons you did not make the team. The coach grants your request and explains that he/she feels that you are not ready to play on the team as a regular player; however, he/she suggests that you become a team supporter this year, with the possibility of being a team player next year, depending on your improvement, dedication, and attitude. The team supporter's position entails attending the practices and games, training with the team, acting as a junior assistant to the coach, learning the game and teamwork from the sidelines, and becoming the team's main source of support and encouragement. You really want to be a player, but you accept the coach's offer and agree to be the team's supporter. The experience and training you will gain this year may enable you to be a great candidate for next year's try-outs.
Benefit: You made a very mature choice by accepting the coach's honest opinion of your current athletic abilities. Agreeing to the terms of being the team supporter this year, with the possibility of becoming a regular team player next year, proved just how committed you are to playing on this team. You may gain valuable experience in team sportsmanship and responsibility, even if you are not chosen as a regular player next year. Congratulations on practicing Self-Serving Strategies.

B.) You decide to yell at the coach. Name calling and profane language is directed to the coach and he/she asks you to leave. You refuse to leave and keep verbally abusing him/her. The coach calls your parents and explains what has happened and asks them to pick you up. When your parents arrive, the coach requests a meeting with you and them. He/she explains that the consequence of your behavior has left him/her no other choice, but to prohibit you from trying-out for this sport in the future. The coach also expressed his/her concern for your temper and lack of respect for authority. Your parents deal with the situation when you all get home.

Consequence: You may have jeopardized the opportunity to play this particular sport in the future. You displayed an extreme amount of disrespect for the coach and his/her assessment of your athletic abilities. Verbal abuse is not an effective way to deal with anger. Finding respectable, healthy ways of expressing yourself in dealing with disappointment may help you in future encounters. This is not an example of using Self-Serving Strategies.

C.) You decide to accept the decision the coach has made, although you are not happy with the results of the team line-up. For the next year, you practice to polish the athletic abilities you have, and learn how to develop new ones. At next year's try-outs you give 110% of all you have and you are chosen to join the team. You are so happy that all of your hard work has paid off.

Benefit: You set a realistic goal for yourself and you backed it up with a plan. You successfully created your own desired outcome by displaying perseverance and good old-fashioned hard work. You knew what you had to do and you did it! Congratulations on a very fine example of practicing Self-Serving Strategies.

Consequence: You may short change yourself by not knowing why you were turned down initially. Requesting a meeting with the coach to discuss exactly why you were not chosen this year to be a team player may have given you additional insight and possibly an opportunity to be a part of the team on a different level. It does not hurt to ask.

This completes Chapter #2: The Sixth Grade. I hope this preview of challenges and dilemmas has provided you with an effective overview of how using Self-Serving Strategies correctly can impact your future in a positive manner. You are personally invited to expand your knowledge of this concept by reviewing the upcoming chapters that depict higher grade levels. Reading and fully comprehending Chapter #9: The Six Bonus Fundamentals may grant you insight into essential subject areas that may benefit your mind, which may enable you to produce your desired goal without hesitation or limitations.

Chapter #3
The Seventh Grade

The seventh grade indicates the average age for young teenagers to experience the onset of puberty. Unexpected challenges may arise as your bodies begin to grow and change. This age group may also provide opportunities of self-discovery, self-development, and self-fulfillment as you learn more about yourself. Peer-pressure may become very prevalent at this grade level; therefore, it may be crucial to learn how to acquire the power of self-definition now to ensure positive outcomes for you in the near future. Enjoy your youth by having fun and establishing healthy friendships. The ten topics presented in this chapter were chosen specifically to help you build positive character traits, deal with peer-pressure, gain more responsibility, and learn how to define yourself. Each illustration is followed by three different answer choices and is accompanied with a possible result described as either a consequence or a benefit for that chosen decision. Please read with the intention of grasping the concept introduced, so that you may practice it in any future predicaments you may soon encounter.

#1.) You are in the seventh grade and have a few really good friends. You have always been included with this group of friends and you all have a great time together. Most recently, for some reason, you were not invited to the last few group outings. In fact, you did not even know your friends went out without you, until you overheard them talking about it at school. You don't know why you are being ousted by people you trusted and considered to be good friends. You want to know what happened, but are not sure if you should confront them directly.
What are your options?

A.) You decide to ask your friends if there is a problem, because you really want to know. You directly ask them why you haven't been invited to the recent group outings and if there is something wrong. Your friends reassure you that there is no problem and that not inviting you was a simple oversight. You begin to feel better, until it happens again. This time you decide not to ask them why, since they were untruthful the first time. Instead, you move forward and focus on developing relationships that exhibit mutual respect and a reciprocal friendship pattern.

Benefit: You really wanted to know "why" your friends have been ousting you and you asked them in a calm, cordial manner; however, their answer eventually did not measure up to their actions and you were hurt again. Trust is the basic foundation for any relationship and when it is broken, it is very difficult to regain. You handled this situation with maturity by not reacting emotionally and by doing what was best for you; thus an excellent example of using Self-Serving Strategies efficiently.

*Sometimes knowing "why" is unimportant, since the answer will never erase the hurtful feelings you had already experienced. It may be better to evaluate just how your friends treated you in the first place and ask yourself if they are the type of friends that deserve your friendship. Then and only then can you acquire the power of self-definition.

B.) You decide to confront them because you are hurt and angry and want some answers. You demand your friends to tell you why they have been ousting you from the group. They react with anger and want to fight. You don't want to fight, so you walk away and go home. You think about how your plan went awry.

Consequence: You confronted your friends with anger, which triggered them to react with anger. Because of your approach, you may never get the answer to your "why" question. This is not an example of using Self-Serving Strategies because resolution may never be reached by using confrontational demands and you may have been physically hurt. *Sometimes knowing "why" is unimportant, since the answer will never erase the hurtful feelings you had already experienced. It may be better to evaluate just how your friends treated you in the first place and ask yourself if they are the type of friends that deserve your friendship. Then and only then, can you acquire the power of self-definition.

C.) You decide to do nothing at the moment; however, you continue to observe their behavior as they exclude you in their future plans. You then decide to take your power back and begin to develop friendships with classmates you have something in common with. You did not feel the need to ask this group of friends "why" because you know you deserve to be mutually respected by all the relationships you choose to develop and nurture.

Benefit: You stayed true to yourself by honoring and valuing your self-worth; which enabled you to make the best possible choice for yourself. Trusting your judgment and making decisions based on your best self-interest may take time to master, but you have made great progress in this example. Not wanting to know "why" because you felt the answer wouldn't matter, was a very mature way of evaluating the situation. Congratulations on practicing Self-Serving Strategies effectively.

#2.) You are in the seventh grade and your best friend has offered to give you a ride home. You accept the offer and meet him/her after school. Unbeknownst to you, his/her brother will be driving you home and not his/her mother or father. You learn that your friend's brother has had his license only for a short time. You are not sure if your parents would have given you permission to accept a ride from an inexperienced driver, so you are confused as to what is the right thing to do. You want to go because you think it will be fun and you don't want to walk home. What are your options?

A.) You decide to accept the ride from your friend's brother. After you get in the car, you notice him drinking a beer while driving. He is underage and you know it is illegal to drink and drive in all fifty states. You are scared and know for a fact that this is wrong and could become very dangerous. You quickly ask to be dropped-off at the nearest curb, get out of the car, and walk home. Although your friend tried to convince you to stay, you had no doubt in your mind that leaving was the right thing to do for yourself. When you get home, you tell your parents what happened and what you did. They are relieved that you asked to get out of the car, but are concerned why you got in the car in the first place. They have a lengthy conversation with you and set some ground rules for safety issues, which helped clear-up the doubt and confusion you were pondering. You are grateful you made the right decision because you value your life.

Consequence: You were in doubt and decided to take the easy way by catching a ride, instead of walking home. Learning to listen to your inner voice when doubt sets in may help keep you safe. Please remember: When in doubt, just say "no, thank you." Your initial choice to accept the ride is not using Self-Serving Strategies because you ignored your doubts and the outcome may have been detrimental to you and your future goals.

Benefit: You put yourself first when you realized how dangerous this ride home may have been. You responded quickly and were very truthful with your parents. You exercised Self-Serving Strategies after you knew the situation may become dangerous and/or life-threatening for you; however, practicing Self-Serving Strategies at the onset of an initial decision may be a wiser choice, since some situations may not afford you an opportunity to change your mind later.

B.) You decide to accept the ride from your friend's brother. After you get in the car, you notice him drinking a beer while driving. He is underage and you know it is illegal for anyone to drink and drive in all fifty states. You are a little scared and you know it is wrong, but you are seeking an adventure. You ask if you guys can go "cruzin" before going home. The driver takes you on a wild ride that eventually catches the police's attention. After getting pulled over, your friend's brother gets arrested and you and your friend are taken to the police station where your parents are called to pick you up.

Consequence: Your decision to go along for the wild ride, when you knew it was wrong and could become dangerous, may have resulted in a life-threatening situation for you. An underage, inexperienced driver who is drinking alcohol while driving may have a high probability of a car accident just waiting to happen. Learning how to curb risk-taking behaviors and thrill seeking adventures may help keep you safe. Your parents may punish you and become less trusting of you for the choices you made in this example. This is not an example of using Self-Serving Strategies because your decision may have resulted in serious injury or even death for you and/or others.

C.) You decide not to accept the ride from your friend's brother because you have doubts. Your friend tries to talk you into going, but you stand firm on your decision and walk home. You arrive safely and fully understand how important it is to keep yourself away from potentially dangerous situations.
Benefit: Your decision not to risk your safety by taking the doubts you had as a serious warning sign was an excellent way of building admirable leadership skills beneficial for your future. You have acquired the power of self-definition and used Self-Serving Strategies efficiently in this example by clearly knowing your true sense of self and by making a decision that best ensured your safety. Congratulations!

#3.) You are in the seventh grade and have been invited to go to a concert with a friend. You know that your parents will not give you permission to go because they think you are too young for the whole concert experience. You really want to go, but are not sure if lying to your parents will be worth the risk. What are your options?

A.) You turn your friend's offer down because you trust your parents judgment and you don't want to lie to them. You don't bother asking your parents because you are sure the answer will be "NO!"
Benefit: Your decision to trust that your parents have your best interest and safety in mind when denying you permission to attend a concert reflects on the close relationship you have built with them; however, you are assuming the answer will still be "NO!" They might have changed their mind if you asked them and provided reasonable transportation plans to meet their concerns. It wouldn't hurt to just ask. Please continue to use wise judgment. Congratulations on a great example of using Self-Serving Strategies.

B.) You really want to go to the concert, so you think it is worth the risk to lie to your parents. You ask them if you could sleep over your friend's house on the night of the concert. They grant you permission since you have slept over there before, they know your friend's parents, and they trust you. A family emergency arises and your father calls your friend's house to speak to you. His/her mother informs your father that you are at a concert and won't be back until nearly midnight. Your parents are both disappointed and concerned regarding your whereabouts. They deal with the family emergency first and then go to your friend's house at midnight to pick you up.

Consequence: You lied to get what you wanted, which created a very fearful situation for your parents because they were unaware of your whereabouts. You may be punished for your decision to deceive your parents and your friend may be disciplined as well for knowingly going along with the plan. It may take some time to rebuild the trusting relationship you once had with your parents. This is not an example of using Self-Serving Strategies because your decision included deceit and dishonesty, which broke your trusting bond with your parents. *Please note: It is very important for your parents to know where you are, what you are doing, and whom you are with at all times.

C.) You really want to go to the concert, so you think it is worth the risk to lie to your parents. You ask them if you could sleep over your friend's house on the night of the concert. They grant you permission since you have slept over there before, they know your friend's parents, and they trust you. At the concert, you begin to feel very overwhelmed with the environment. You become fascinated with the way older teenagers and young adults are dressed. You see many tattoos, body piercing in unusual places, brightly colored hair, peculiar clothing (leather, holes, dyed, etc.), and a lot of silver jewelry. Concentrating on enjoying the concert becomes difficult with all these distractions and influences. After the concert, you go back to your friend's house to sleep over; however, you have a hard time falling asleep because the images of those people keep popping up in your head. The next day you go home and do not get caught for lying to your parents. You now understand why your parents thought you were too young for the whole concert experience.

Consequence: Your decision to attend a concert without your parent's permission may create a negative experience for you that may result in unfavorable flashbacks in the future. Although you did not get caught, you may need to keep covering up this lie if the subject becomes relevant. Living a life free from limitations and negative memories may allow you to reach your full potential. Please learn to trust your parents. After all, they have life experience and have learned life lessons. This is not an example of using Self-Serving Strategies because you chose to lie to get your way. You also put yourself in an environment that could have been unsafe for you. Respecting your parent's judgments on decisions they make is invaluable to your relationship with them. *Remember, they will always have your best interest and safety at heart.

#4.) You are in the seventh grade and have a teacher that isn't very nice to you. According to your own personal experiences, he/she has been downright mean to you. You feel that he/she is biased, grades you unfairly, and speaks to you harshly. Classmates have also witnessed his/her behavior. You want your teacher to treat you cordially and fairly, but you don't think anyone will believe you. What are your options?

A.) You decide to treat this teacher with no respect. You answer him/her rudely, interrupt him/her when he/she is talking, and you continuously speak negatively about him/her. The situation escalates and the teacher becomes very annoyed with your behavior and refers you to the vice principal to be disciplined. In the vice principal's office you express your frustrations and negative experiences you've had with this teacher. The vice principal is not convinced of your accusations because he/she thinks you are lying to help excuse your own behavior. You have a difficult time being perceived as truthful.

Consequence: Your decision to retaliate backfired on you. The old saying "two wrongs don't make a right" rings true in this example. The vice principal may never believe your statements of unfairness and you may be disciplined for your disrespectful behavior. Please learn and practice effective communication, which displays mutual respect and an opportunity to express your concerns and experiences in a safe environment. This is not an example of using Self-Serving Strategies because your choice was revengeful and was meant to hurt someone.

B.) You decide to tell your parents how your teacher has been treating you. They request a conference with this teacher AND the principal. At the meeting, you feel safe to share your negative experiences and disclose the names of classmates that have witnessed this teacher's behavior.

Benefit: Your decision to openly and honestly express your feelings, frustrations, and fears with your parents was an effective, mature approach in dealing with this situation. Your parent's trust in you prompted them to take immediate action. By not resorting to name-calling or bad-mouthing the teacher to anyone, you displayed professionalism and respect for authority. Being validated and heard for your concerns in a diplomatic manner may have taught you an invaluable life lesson, regardless of the outcome. Learning how to voice your discrepancies with people of authority is difficult to master because emotions and reactions need to be avoided. Knowing that you did not deserve to be treated unfairly and rudely by a teacher, disclosing the information properly, and keeping the situation private were all great examples of using Self-Serving Strategies proficiently. You also acquired the power of self-definition by knowing your self-worth and by not allowing anyone to belittle you. Congratulations!

C.) You decide to speak very negatively about this teacher. The gossip spreads throughout the school and it has become a nuisance on campus. The vice principal investigates the situation and discovers that the original "rumor" was started by you. In your meeting with him/her you explain that your statements about the teacher are real and not rumors. You go on to illustrate your uncomfortable experiences and provide names of witnesses. The vice principal takes a proactive approach to determine the facts of your accusations. You are disciplined for creating a hostile environment on campus.

Consequence: Your choice to speak negatively about this teacher was an immature approach in trying to deal with your frustrations and negative experiences. It may have been difficult for the vice principal to believe you, based on your behavior. The disciplinary decision may include suspension, detention, and/or a Chapter 19 violation. The action taken may be documented on your school record. Please learn and practice effective communication, which displays mutual respect and an opportunity to express your concerns and experiences in a safe environment. This is not an example of using Self-Serving Strategies because your decision created a hostile environment on school campus and your purpose was to humiliate the teacher.

#5.) You are in the seventh grade and your parents have given you some money to purchase your school supplies and P.E. uniforms for this school year. Their plan is to give you more responsibility by learning money management and being trustworthy. You are up for the challenge, but you are tempted to buy other things. What are your options?

A.) You decide to curb your temptation to buy other things. Instead you search for the school supplies you need in the weekly sales, budget the money wisely, purchase everything you need (including the P.E. uniforms), and give the change back to your parents. You have all the supplies and materials you need to create a positive learning environment for yourself.

Benefit: Your decision to be responsible and trustworthy displayed maturity. We can't always get what we want, when we want it. It may become especially difficult to avoid temptation when money is handed to you, but intended for a specific purpose. Your choice also gave you an opportunity to build positive character traits beneficial to your future. Your parents may become more trusting of you, which may result in more responsibility in future tasks. This is an excellent example of using Self-Serving Strategies efficiently because you benefited from doing the right thing, which may produce great learning outcomes for you.

B.) You decide to buy something special for yourself with most of the money. With the change, you buy the cheapest school supplies you can find. Since you spent all the money your parents gave you, you can't buy the P.E. uniforms. School becomes frustrating for you because your school supplies break easily and you constantly need to ask classmates to borrow theirs. You also have had to come up with different excuses for not having the proper P.E. uniform. Your P.E. teacher gives you a deadline to comply with the school rules.

Consequence: Your decision to use most of the money on something special for yourself was irresponsible. Your choice has led you to create excuses and lies to cover-up why you don't have the proper P.E. uniforms. It's just a matter of time before your parents are notified and the truth surfaces. They may become less trusting of you and reduce your responsibilities, since you may have proven how irresponsible you can be. Your classmates may become irritated with you because of your continuous borrowing of their school supplies. This is not an example of using Self-Serving Strategies because your choice was selfish, deceitful, dishonest, and you suffered from it. You may curtail your education by not having the proper school supplies handy, since these items are considered your learning tools.

C.) You decide to buy something special for yourself with most of the money. With the change, you buy the cheapest school supplies you can find. Since you don't have any cash left to buy the P.E. uniforms, you tell your parents you need more money. Your parents ask for all the receipts for the purchases you made. After everything is calculated, they simply ask you "where did all the money go?"

Consequence: Your decision to use most of the money to buy something special for yourself was irresponsible. Asking your parents for money was a little gutsy. Your parents may become less trusting of you and may punish you for the choices you made. It may take a long time for you to regain their trust. This is not an example of using Self-Serving Strategies because your choice was selfish, deceitful, and dishonest. These are all characteristics that WILL NOT benefit your future positively.

#6.) You are in the seventh grade and your parents have recently divorced. You spend time with each parent, but nearly dread being alone with either one of them. When you are with your mother, she speaks very negatively about your father and vice versa. You don't like the uncomfortable feeling of being caught in the middle of their problems. You love both your parents, but you don't know how to deal with this situation. What are your options?

A.) You decide the best way to deal with this uncomfortable situation is to just agree with the parent you are with at the time. Although you feel you are caught in the middle, you think it is worth it because both of your parents are now happy.
Consequence: Your choice to sacrifice your own emotional needs for the sake of your parent's happiness is not in your best self-interest. Your parents may be acting very immaturely because they are angry. You need to understand that your parents are adults; therefore, you are not responsible for their happiness. You may have created a false sense of trust with each parent when you agreed with their comments about one another. This is not an example of using Self-Serving Strategies because your sacrifice may cause emotional distress and psychological problems for you in the future.

B.) You decide the best way to deal with this uncomfortable situation is to just agree with the parent you are with at the time and try to manipulate them, out of guilt, for extra gifts and money. Your plan works and you get really cool gifts and a lot of cash from both parents.
Consequence: Your decision to take advantage of the situation by using guilt to attain gifts and money from your parents was very manipulative and dishonest. These negative behaviors may become

stepping stones for other unfavorable character traits, which may affect your future plans and goals. Materialistically benefiting in this situation by using your parents is definitely not an example of using Self-Serving Strategies. Your choice was not clever, but very selfish. You may ultimately hurt yourself and your future if you continue to make decisions similar to this one. Please consider focusing and displaying positive behavioral patterns.

C.) You decide to ask for a family meeting. You carefully explain how you feel and your parents are grateful for your honesty. They admit they were unaware of how their actions were affecting you and apologize for their behavior. You suggest that the time spent with each of them be private and with no negative reference about the other parent. Your parents agree to your suggestion and visits with them become memorable and pleasurable.

Benefit: You stayed true to yourself by expressing your frustrations and needs to your parents in a safe, respectful manner. You displayed leadership skills, which is an admirable character trait, by requesting a family meeting, explaining your position, and offering a resolution to your dilemma. Your parents may become more trustworthy of you since you chose to be honest with them. This is an excellent example of using Self-Serving Strategies because you did what was best for you, and you created a comfortable environment for yourself, which may benefit your future favorably. Congratulations!

#7.) You are in the seventh grade and male. You have your very first real girlfriend. You really like her, but are confused about what to do and how to act. Your guy friends give you unsolicited advice on what you are supposed to do, but you are not sure if treating her in that way is acceptable. You like your first girlfriend and want to keep her, but you are feeling confused and pressured from your friends on what to do. What are your options?

A.) You decide to ask your father for advice. He has a heart-to-heart talk with you and explains the rules, purpose, and rewards of having a girlfriend. First he tells you the rules are very simple:

Always treat her with respect. Really listen to her when she expresses herself. Put her before your friends. Trust and believe in her. Secondly, he explains the real purpose of having a girlfriend is an opportunity to get to know her and to share special experiences with. Your father then states the most valued reward is the gift of learning how to care for someone else unconditionally. You take his advice and slowly develop a healthy romantic relationship with your first girlfriend. You treat her respectfully and are there when she needs you. You don't allow your friends to influence your decisions or pressure you into displaying inappropriate behavior.

Benefit: Your choice to ask your father for advice, instead of following your friend's coaxing, was very admirable and smart. You decided to ask a person who definitely has experience with women and knows the proper way to treat them. Because you sought out the information for yourself, evaluated it, and made a decision that best suited your self-interest respectively, you acquired the power of self-definition. Congratulations! This is also an excellent example of using Self-Serving Strategies proficiently.

B.) You decide to be honest with your new girlfriend and explain to her how you are not sure of what to do. You both have a discussion of expectations and begin to negotiate the terms of your relationship. You are both in agreement of those terms, which will remain private, and begin your romantic relationship with trust and respect.

Benefit: Your decision to be honest with your new girlfriend showed maturity and humility, two very favorable characteristics to attain. You successfully negotiated the terms of your relationship with trust and respect, which displayed excellent communication skills. Your relationship has the potential to develop into something very special for both of you. Congratulations on displaying Self-Serving Strategies and acquiring the power of self-definition.

C.) You decide to follow your friend's advice and tell your new girlfriend how things are going to be and demand her to do exactly what you want her to do! She doesn't appreciate being disrespected and tells you that she is not willing to compromise herself and her values for your so-called demands. She breaks-up with you on the spot. You are confused because you thought you did what you were supposed to do based on your friend's advice.

Consequence: Your decision to follow your friend's advice resulted in losing your first girlfriend BEFORE the relationship had a chance of starting. This is an example of becoming a follower, which may influence your future negatively. You also disrespected a girl you liked because you were not informed properly on how to establish a healthy, romantic relationship with her. It is your responsibility to seek advice and information from people who have real experience in the subject matter. Relying on friends, who probably never had real girlfriends before, for advice has proven to be unwise. Sorry, this is not an example of using Self-Serving Strategies correctly because your best self-interest was not served and your actions disrespected your girlfriend. Please consider reviewing "Romantic Relationship Wise" and "Dating Wise" in Chapter #1: The Wise Segments for information and advice on how to develop healthy relationships.

#8.) You are in the seventh grade and your parents have always used spanking as a form of punishment. Lately your father has been punishing you severely, leaving visible bruises and lacerations, and you are afraid of him. You try to make sure he doesn't get mad at you because you don't want to get hit anymore. Fear overwhelms your life and you are having a difficult time concentrating on school and other activities. You want your father to stop hitting you, but you are afraid of taking action or telling anyone. What are your options?

A.) You decide not to tell anyone, tolerate the pain, and keep the situation a secret. You begin to hide the bruises and make excuses for any visible scares. You try very hard not to show your anger, but your emotions are triggered easily. Pent-up anger begins to surface and people are becoming uncomfortable in your presence. You think that you created a solution to your secret problem, but are now feeling alienated and alone.

Consequence: Your decision to protect your dad and suffer from his continuous physical abuse did not result in a favorable outcome for you. In fact, you have suffered more by not creating a solution in your best self-interest. You may need extensive counseling for the abuse you have suffered and you may need to learn anger management skills to cope with your built-up anger issues. This is not an example of using Self-Serving Strategies because your choice did not benefit you or your future positively. *Note: The father in this example was not using spanking as a form of punishment. His actions are classified as physical abuse. When a child has fear, anger, and noticeable bruises and scares, he/she is being physically abused and NOT spanked. Please get help because you deserve to live in a safe environment free from any abusive components or experiences.

B.) You decide to tell a school counselor because you are scared of telling your mom. The counselor examines your bruises and scares and reports the abuse to the proper authorities. An investigation is conducted and it has been determined that your household is unsafe for you to live in. You are placed in a foster home and receive the care and counseling you need to help heal from your ordeal. Your father is very upset with you, but your mother seems to be relieved.

Benefit: Your choice, although difficult to make, was made in your best self-interest. Concentrating on you and creating a solution that immediately stopped the abuse is an excellent example of using Self-Serving Strategies proficiently. Being placed in a caring, loving foster home and receiving the help you need to overcome the abuse you have suffered, may have provided you with the best possible outcome that may benefit your future in a positive manner. Congratulations on putting yourself first. *Note: If your father receives the help he needs to control his anger and admits to his abusive actions, he may come to understand why you needed to get help.

C.) You decide to confront your father. You demand that he stop hitting you. He gets angrier and hits you with his fist. You fight back and become seriously injured. You need immediate medical attention, but your father is afraid to take you to the hospital because he can't explain your injuries without incriminating himself. Since he knows that your injuries are not life-threatening, he keeps you at home and out of school until they have healed. You return to school with unexplained scares, so you make up a story to cover the truth. You decided to protect your father because you are more afraid of him now.

Consequence: Your choice to confront an already angry person was not very wise. Your decision to demand your father to stop abusing you resulted in you getting seriously injured. You may think you did the right thing by standing-up for yourself, but your choice did not serve your best self- interest because there was no solution forthcoming and you got seriously hurt. Sorry, this is not an example of using Self-Serving Strategies correctly. Please consider your safety first when evaluating a situation before making a decision. *Note: If you don't seek help for the abuse you are suffering from, you might continue the cycle of abuse/violence in your future relationships. Pent-up anger and resentment are key factors in a person who chooses physical, interpersonal violence as a way of dealing with his/her anger. Experiencing anger and pain (physical and/or emotional) are also indicators and precursors for addiction because a person may want to ignore his/her problems and become numb from them. "Addiction Wise" in Chapter #1: The Wise Segments may provide you with insight, information, and advice on how to cope with your circumstantial situation. It is of utmost importance for you to seek help from a reputable counselor or doctor to heal yourself from this pain. Please get the help you need now in order to live in a safe environment that enables you to be a productive member of society.

#9.) You are in the seventh grade and have been working hard to achieve a certain short term goal, but can't seem to accomplish it. Although you have tried your very best, you just can't seem to achieve it. You really want to reach your goal, but think it may be time to give up. What are your options?

A.) You decide that it is time to give-up. You have accepted the fact that you probably will never reach your goal, so you stop concentrating on trying to achieve it. You feel disappointed with yourself; however, you don't second guess your decision. Life resumes as usual for you.

Consequence: Your choice to give-up on your goal was probably made out of frustration and constant disappointment and not on your talent abilities. Sometimes making a decision subjectively (based on emotions and opinions) and not objectively (based on facts and experience) may be made hastily. Believing in yourself and having confidence to achieve any goal are key factors in your ability to succeed. This is not an example of using Self-Serving Strategies because you may always wonder if you could have reached your goal if you continued to try your best, which may result in a negative experience for you.

B.) You decide to keep trying to achieve your goal. You continue to produce your absolute best work and concentrate on your ultimate goal. Focus and commitment overshadow doubt and uncertainty. After time and a lot of hard work, your goal is achieved.

Benefit: Your choice to continue working at achieving your goal was an excellent example of perseverance and diligence. Remaining focused and committed until your ultimate goal was reached displayed determination and confidence. Your choice provided you with an opportunity to build leadership skills. Congratulations on all your hard work, practicing Self-Serving Strategies, and acquiring the power of self-definition.

C.) You decide to keep trying to achieve your goal. You can't seem to understand why you haven't been able to achieve your goal thus far, so you ask someone who has expertise in the field you are trying to master. He/she reviews and evaluates your progress and provides you with suggestions for improvement. You choose to use his/her advice and make the proper changes. You are very proud and believe it is the best work you have ever produced.

Benefit: Your decision to ask an expert for his/her advice has proven to be a very wise choice. Accepting his/her recommendations for improvement was done with humility and an open mind. Your actions displayed maturity and confidence. Whether or not you actually reach your ultimate goal is inconsequential because you know that you produced your best work ever; therefore, your best self-interest was already served. Congratulations on exhibiting the use of Self-Serving Strategies in a great example of advocating for yourself and acquiring the power of self-definition.

#10.) You are in the seventh grade and want to make some money. You know that you don't want to actually work hard to earn the money doing odd jobs in the neighborhood. After carefully considering your limited options because of your young age and unwillingness to work hard, you realize that newspaper vending machines use the honor system when dispensing the newspapers. This basically means that people put their money in the machine and take only the amount of papers they actually paid for. Since the machine has no way to prevent a person from taking more, you suddenly have a great idea! You pay for only one newspaper, but take more papers and resell them in the neighborhood. You know this is stealing, but you want to make money the easy way. What are your options?

A.) You decide to go along with your idea. You buy only one paper from a few different newspaper vending machines around town, but take more. You stand on a corner of your neighborhood and resell the newspapers. A week goes by and things are great. You make enough money to buy what you wanted, so you stop the next day. You never get caught and you go on with your daily routine and responsibilities.

Consequence: Your choice to steal newspapers then resell them to make easy money was very dishonest and deceitful. The behavior you displayed may be a precursor to higher risk-taking theft adventures that may become detrimental for you and your future plans and goals. Although you did not get caught, you still committed a crime. Your luck may soon run its course if you decide to continue on this destructive path. This is definitely not an example of using Self-Serving Strategies because your choice was dishonest and unlawful.

B.) You decide to go along with your own idea. You buy only one paper from a few different newspaper vending machines around town, but take more. You stand on a corner of your neighborhood and resell the newspapers. Things go smoothly for about a week, until the person monitoring the vending machines witnesses your devious plan. He/she reports the theft to the "BIG" boss and the police are called to investigate the theft. You are taken to the police station for questioning. Since you are a minor and this was your first offense, charges are not filed and you are released into your parent's custody.

Consequence: Your choice to steal newspapers then resell them to make easy money was very dishonest and deceitful. The behavior you displayed may be a precursor to higher risk-taking theft adventures that may become detrimental for you and your future plans and goals. Your parents may be less trusting of you and they may punish you for the crime you committed. The newspaper agency may require you to pay restitution at an estimated cost at their judgment. This is definitely not an example of using Self-Serving Strategies because your choice was dishonest and unlawful.

C.) You decide to scratch your idea because you know committing a crime to make easy money is wrong and not worth any consequence that may result. You change your attitude and decide to work for the money you want instead. After asking a few neighbors for part-time work after school and on weekends, you find a steady job. You honestly earn money by old-fashioned hard work.

Benefit: You stayed true to yourself by doing what you knew was the right thing. Not willing to compromise yourself for the sake of making easy money was very admirable. By creating a favorable, honest outcome for yourself, you displayed and executed Self-Serving Strategies effectively. This example gave you an opportunity to build leadership skills essential and beneficial for your future plans and goals. You also acquired the power of self-definition by realizing who you are and making decisions that reflect your own values.

This completes Chapter #3: The Seventh Grade. I hope the subject matters chosen for this chapter were able to provide you with a clear understanding of how to use Self-Serving Strategies correctly. A few examples exemplified how you can acquire the power of self-definition. It may take more practice to learn how to integrate Self-Serving Strategies into your everyday life, so feel free to read ahead in the upcoming grade level chapters to gain more experience. Please remember this book was created for the benefit of your future. Reviewing Chapter #9: The Six Bonus Fundamentals may give you the knowledge to live proficiently by avoiding and/or handling negative experiences that may cause possible flashbacks and limitations for you.

Chapter #4
The Eighth Grade

The eighth grade may represent significant upcoming changes for all you teenagers. As a student attending a middle/intermediate school, you will be an example for the lower grade levels as they search for guidance and learn from your achievements and/or challenges. This year may also be the last time your friends remain in the same group. High school enrollment consists of the blending of middle/intermediate schools within a district; therefore, opportunities to establish new friendships may be evident and forthcoming. Enjoy your last year of middle/intermediate school by having fun with your close friends and keeping an open mind about next year's adjustments in high school.

These particular topics and subject matters in this chapter were specifically chosen to provide a diverse variety of situational dilemmas that include various temptations and inappropriate behavioral experiences. Many situations involve learning personal and civic responsibility. I hope the answer choices given will help you to understand how the concept of using Self-Serving Strategies correctly, effectively, and proficiently may benefit your future goals. Each of the ten examples is followed by three different answer choices and is concluded with either a consequence or a benefit as a possible outcome for that chosen option. Please read with compassion and empathy, as some teenagers actually have experienced, or are currently experiencing, some of these real-life dilemmas.

#1.) You are in the eighth grade and have won second place in a school wide contest. Before the awards ceremony, you learn that the first place winner cheated in the competition. You don't think this is fair, but are not sure of what to do. What are your options?

A.) You decide to bring it to the attention of the authorities. The awards ceremony is held up for nearly thirty minutes, while an informal investigation is conducted. Since you can't provide proof of your accusation, your second place standing remains. You accept your award, but you are not happy because you don't think justice was served. Your negative attitude and angry demeanor does not go unnoticed by the administration, faculty, parents, and students. People seem to be annoyed with you for making them wait. You strongly believe that you were robbed out of winning first place by a cheater.

Consequence: You believed that you had the right to tell the authorities what you knew about the first place winner; however, the way you did it may need some improving. It may take practice learning how to evaluate situations to come up with the best possible plan of action. Learning when and how to voice your convictions may provide you with leadership skills invaluable for your future. Although you stood-up for yourself, the bad attitude and anger you displayed at the ceremony was disrespectful for not only the audience witnessing it, but for the school administration as well; therefore, this is not an example of using Self-Serving Strategies correctly.

B.) You decide to accept your second place award gracefully and without prejudice. You go on with your life and don't think twice about it. Although the first place winner was never caught for cheating in the contest, you know that cheaters never really win in the game called life. You are proud of your of achievement.

Benefit: Your decision to accept your award without disclosing any accusations of cheating was a mature approach in dealing with the situation. Being proud of yourself for accomplishing second place in a school wide contest is in itself very admirable. This is a great example of using Self-Serving Strategies proficiently because you concentrated on doing what was best for you, without worrying about someone else's dishonest behavior. Congratulations!

C.) You decide to accept your second place award gracefully and without prejudice. You go on with your life and don't think twice about it because you are proud of achieving second place. After a few weeks have passed, evidence surfaced questioning the authenticity of the first place contestant winner. He/she gets caught for cheating and a special assembly is arranged to redistribute the awards. You receive the first place winning award for the contest.

Benefit: Your decision to accept your award without disclosing any accusations of cheating was a mature approach in dealing with the situation. By not involving yourself in a pursuit of justice, an investigation was able to be conducted without bias or prejudice, which resulted in a favorable outcome for you; however, being proud of yourself for accomplishing second place in a school wide contest is in itself very admirable. This is a great example of using Self-Serving Strategies proficiently because you concentrated on doing what was best for you, without worrying about someone else's dishonest behavior. Congratulations!

#2.) You are in the eighth grade and have an important homework assignment due in a few days that you haven't started yet. The report requires in depth research complete with a bibliography, proper citations, and a minimum of five pages. You express how overwhelmed and frustrated you are to a classmate and he/she suggests that you simply buy a finished report and claim it as your own. You want to relax and not worry about this assignment anymore, but you know that buying a paper and submitting it as your own work is plagiarism. What are your options?

A.) You decide not to cheat and devote the next few days to starting and finishing your research paper. You ask for help from your teacher and the school librarian. You try your best, although your time is limited. When you are done, you turn your paper in on the due date. You don't feel confident because you know you could have done a better job if you didn't procrastinate; however, you are proud that you didn't take the easy, dishonest way out by cheating.

Benefit: You stayed true to yourself by not allowing your stress level to convince you that cheating is okay. You created a plan of action and executed it successfully. Asking for help and doing the best you could for the allotted time remaining was an excellent way to deal with the pressure of meeting your deadline. This is an example of using Self-Serving Strategies because you produced your own work; however, please be careful not to let procrastination become a habit, since it may affect your future negatively.

Consequence: Because you waited to begin your assignment and you knew you did not submit your best work, your grade may be affected; thus, not practicing Self-Serving Strategies. Allowing yourself time to prepare and produce work at your fullest potential, may provide you with great confidence and practice in developing successful study habits.

B.) You decide to buy the paper and turn it in on the due date. You don't think you will get caught, so you relax and enjoy the next few days. You receive your graded paper and notice the less-than-favorable letter grade on it. You can't seem to understand why you didn't earn a better grade. You scan thru the grading criteria and realize the missing components of your paper. Because you did not take the time to read the report before you submitted it, you were not able to notice its incomplete sections. Although you did not get caught for cheating, your posted grade for this assignment reduced your overall class average grade. You will need to work diligently to bring your grade back up.

Consequence: Your decision to cheat was not only dishonest, but it resulted in you earning a bad grade. It may take some time, and a lot of hard work, to bring your class average back to where it was. You may think that you got away with plagiarism because you did not get busted, but you will always know what you did was wrong, which may result in a negative experience and/or memory for you. If you did get caught for cheating, you may have been expelled because schools take plagiarism very seriously. This is definitely not an example of practicing Self-Serving Strategies because cheating may impact your future negatively.

C.) You decide to buy the paper and turn it in on the due date. You don't think you will get caught, so you relax for the next few days. The following week you are called to the principal's office. You calmly report to the office were you are greeted by your parents. The meeting begins by the principal asking you where you got your paper. You are scared, but act innocent. After a few minutes, you realized how profound the evidence is against you, so you confess to buying the paper from someone you didn't know.

Consequence: You got caught for plagiarism and you may be expelled from school under the Chapter 19 violations for cheating and dishonest academic conduct. Your parents may enforce their own punishment for the choices you made and they may become less trusting of you. If you are not expelled from school, you may receive suspension or another form of disciplinary action. You probably earned a "0" for that assignment, if you remain enrolled that school. This is not an example of practicing Self-Serving Strategies because cheating is dishonest and it impacted your future negatively in this situation.

#3.) You are in the eighth grade and want to make some extra money to buy something special. Your friend tells you that gambling is a quick way to make money. He/she introduces you to a few people who gamble regularly; they shoot dice and play cards after school and on weekends. You know that gambling is illegal, but you want to make some quick cash. What are your options?

A.) You decide to try gambling and you lose everything. Now you are broke and learned a valuable lesson; gambling is not worth the risk of losing your money. You resort to the old-fashioned way of honestly earning money from hard work.

Consequence: Your decision to risk your money by gambling did not pay-off for you. Losing the money you initially had may have helped you realize the true value of it. You gave into temptation hoping that there would be a huge pay-out, but instead you were left broke and disappointed. The only way you can guarantee making any HONEST money is simply earning it by hard work. This choice is not an example of using Self-Serving Strategies because it is illegal; however your reaction to the lessoned learned was a step in the right direction. Please continue to earn your money honestly.

B.) You decide to try gambling and win a lot of money. You continue to gamble and win for the next couple of days. You are so happy because you have won so much money and you can buy the things you want. On the way to the store, your friend tells you that there will be a double or nothing gambling game taking place in a few hours. You weigh the odds of winning and decide to take the chance, banking on your recent winning streak. You go and put everything you have down on the game with confidence that you will win and win big. Well, you lose and lose big instead. You are broke and feel very depressed because you can't buy the things you want anymore.

Consequence: Your decision allowed you to experience the highs and lows of gambling. Because you liked the thrilling risk of gambling and the enjoyment of winning, this choice may lead you to develop an addiction for it. You lost all your money. Please note that nothing good can ever come from doing something bad. Gambling is illegal in most states and underage gambling is illegal in all states. If you don't stop gambling and cut your losses now, you may get caught and be arrested in the near future. This is not an example of using Self-Serving Strategies because it is illegal!

C.) You decide to find work in your neighborhood and earn the money you need to buy the things you want. After searching for a few weeks, you find a job that fits your schedule and begin working hard. You save your money until you have enough to purchase that something special you've been waiting to buy. You feel proud of yourself for earning your money the honest way.

Benefit: You did not give into temptation or try to make money the fast, easy way. Instead you created a plan of action and followed through with it by relying on yourself to earn the money honestly. Congratulations on a great example of practicing Self-Serving Strategies and acquiring the power of Self-definition.

#4.) You are in the eighth grade and have an after school job three times a week in your neighborhood (yard work, babysitting, cleaning houses, washing cars, etc.) Your friends have invited you to hang-out after school on a work day. You want to go and have fun, but you have responsibilities to adhere to and people depending on you. What are your options?

A.) You decide to tell your friends that you need to go to work. Then you report to work on time and do the best job you possibly can. The next day in school your friends tell you how much fun they had. It doesn't bother you because you know that going to work was the right, responsible thing to do and that there will be other times to hang-out with your friends when it fits your schedule.

Benefit: You stayed true to yourself by keeping an agreement with your employer to report to work when you are scheduled to do so. This is a very responsible way of developing a good work ethic. You may receive a favorable recommendation from your boss, when it is time for you to progress to another job. Although you wanted to go with your friends, you remained focused and did not allow temptation or peer pressure to influence your decision. Congratulations on practicing Self-Serving Strategies and acquiring the power of self-definition.

B.) You decide to go with your friends instead of going to work. You have a great time and don't regret your decision. That night your boss calls you and asks you where you were? You act as though you didn't know you were scheduled to work. After pleading with him/her for a second chance to prove you can be responsible, he/she gives in. You keep your job.

Consequence: Your decision to go and have fun with your friends at the risk of possibly losing your job for not showing up was very irresponsible. Although your boss agreed to give you a second chance, he/she may be less trusting of you. You may think that you got away with your dishonest excuse for not reporting to work, but lies almost always surface. When and if the truth does come out, you probably will be fired. Taking your job for granted and lying to get what you want are unfavorable characteristics, which may prove to be detrimental for your future. These behaviors may lead you to experiment with higher risk-taking and dishonest temptations. This is not an example of using Self-Serving Strategies because your choice displayed irresponsibility and dishonesty.

C.) You decide to go with your friends instead of going to work. You have a great time and don't regret your decision. That night your boss calls you and asks you where you were. You act as though you didn't know you were scheduled to work. After pleading with him/her for a second chance to prove you can be responsible, he/she decides to fire you and informs you when you can pick-up your last check. Since your ex-boss fired you for not showing up for work, asking for a positive recommendation from him/her for future employment is out of the question.

Consequence: Your decision to go and have fun with your friends cost you your job. After school jobs are not easy to come by for teens your age and you took yours for granted by disrespecting your boss by being unreliable. Earning your own money for personal use is very gratifying and empowering. It may take a while for you to find employment in your neighborhood because people tend to share their negative experiences with others. You may have developed a reputation for being untrustworthy and irresponsible, which may prevent otherwise willing employers to take a chance with you. This is not an example of using Self-Serving Strategies because you lied and you lost your job; two variables that won't benefit your future positively in any manner.

#5.) You are in the eighth grade and a classmate has dared you to light firecrackers on school campus. He/she wants you to light them during a school wide assembly taking place in the cafeteria the next day. You know that popping firecrackers are illegal (except on designated holidays), but you are tempted to complete this dare for the thrill of it. What are your options?

A.) You decide not to do the dare, but you know the person who has agreed to complete it and you don't tell anyone. He/she lights the firecrackers the next day during the school wide assembly. The unexpected popping noise scared many students and faculty members. People were injured as they rushed out of the cafeteria. One person was burnt from being in close proximity of the firecrackers. After everyone was safe and the injured people were cared for, the principal announced over the intercom that the police were going to conduct a thorough investigation and that the culprits were going to be disciplined to the full extent of the law.

Consequence: Your decision not to participate in the dare was great; however, not telling anyone on campus was irresponsible. There is a purpose for laws. It is your civic duty to report any unlawful activity, especially when it may be dangerous to others, as soon as the information becomes available to you. You may be reprimanded by the principal or vice-principal for not coming forward, if your name surfaces in the investigation. Although you did not complete the dare, this is still not an example of using Self-Serving Strategies because you did not tell anyone the dangerous plan, which resulted in innocent people getting hurt. Please use better judgment in the future.

B.) You decide not to do the dare and you report the pending plans to a school counselor. He/she asked you a few questions then forwarded the information to the vice-principal. The students involved were dealt with and their firecrackers were confiscated. You know that everyone will be safe attending tomorrow's assembly.
Benefit: You made the best possible choice for everyone, including yourself. Congratulations for taking responsibility by reporting the upcoming dangerous dare to your school counselor. You also practiced great leadership skills, which is very admirable and may benefit your future positively. This is an excellent example of using Self-Serving Strategies proficiently. Once again, Congratulations!

C.) You decide to take the dare because you are a thrill seeker. The next day during the assembly you light the firecrackers and throw them up in the air and then run. They land on a table in the back of cafeteria. Luckily no one was nearby. People were scared, but no injuries were reported. Since you have never done something like this before, you did not know that running away only draws attention to you; therefore, you were caught almost instantly. You were taken to the office. The police and your parents were called.
Consequence: Your decision to complete this dare for the thrill of it, although you knew it was illegal and dangerous, was very irresponsible. People could have been seriously injured, if the firecrackers landed in a populated place. You may be sanctioned with Chapter 19 violations, which may include being arrested

61

and/or being suspended. Your parents may also enforce their own punishment for your actions. This thrill seeking behavior you displayed may lead you to seek higher risk-taking dares, if it is not curbed and transformed into healthier approaches to feed your adventurous nature. Please learn the concept of Self-Serving Strategies and how to effectively use it when faced with challenging situations for the betterment of your future.

#6.) You are in the eighth grade and a close friend has run away from home. He/she has asked you to hide him/her in your bedroom for a few days. You want to be a good friend, but you know it is wrong and that his/her parents would be very worried. What are your options?

A.) You decide not to hide your runaway friend; however, you do invite him/her over your house after school to discuss his/her frustrations and problems that led to him/her leaving home. When you get to your house, you explain the situation to your parents and they advise your friend to call home and get permission for being at their house. His/her parents were very worried and agree to grant your friend a cooling-off period. Your friend has permission to stay until after dinner and will be picked-up by his/her parents before 8:00 p.m. You spend the time talking about his/her problems because you wanted to be a good, supportive friend. Before you know it, it's time for dinner. Your friend's parents come shortly after to pick him/her up. It is now nearly 8:00 p.m. and you have just realized that you haven't done any of your homework or your daily chores. You were too busy being consumed with your friend's parental relationship problems to focus on your own responsibilities. Now, you must complete everything before going to bed.

Consequence: Yes, it was great that you decided not to hide your runaway friend; however, allowing him/her to consume all of your time delayed the starting and completion of your daily responsibilities. This resulted in putting your own needs last, which is not an example of using Self-Serving Strategies effectively. Being a supportive friend does not need to include self-sacrifice.

If you did your chores while listening to your friend vent about his/her problems, then you would have been able to manage your time wisely and get some of your daily duties accomplished. Being open about your friend's situation with your parents was a great example of effective communication.

B.) You decide not to hide your runaway friend. You advise him/her to discuss the family's problems with his/her parents to prevent worrisome emotions. You explain to him/her that you are willing to provide support as a good friend, but are not willing to harbor a runaway in your bedroom for any amount of time. You have daily routines and responsibilities that you need to focus on and therefore, don't have the time or energy to get involved in your friend's parental relationship problems; however, when he/she wants to talk, you offer to listen as long as it doesn't interfere with your duties or consume your time.

Benefit: You stayed true to yourself by being a healthy, supportive friend without compromising your values. You openly told your friend what you were and were not willing to do for him/her, which was a great example of effective communication. You stayed focused on your own responsibilities, while still providing support to your friend. This is a great example of balancing the things that matter most to you efficiently. Congratulations on practicing Self-Serving Strategies and acquiring the power of self-definition by setting boundaries and staying focused.

C.) You decide to be a good friend and hide your runaway friend in your bedroom. You sneak him/her food and entertainment materials for nearly three days, until you get caught by your parents. They call your friend's parents, who have been worried sick and inform them of their son/daughter's whereabouts for the last three days. Your friend is picked-up and their family deals with their problems. You feel relieved because you have been a nervous wreck for the past few days.

Consequence: Your decision to harbor your runaway friend because you thought that it was what a good friend should do, although you knew it was wrong, is actually giving into peer pressure. When a friend asks you to do something wrong, especially when it serves him/her only, it may be time to get a new friend. "Friendship Wise" in Chapter #1: The Wise Segments offers definitions and examples of healthy and unhealthy friendships, along with suggestions on evaluating and dissolving relationships for the betterment of your future. Please consider reviewing that chapter for clarity. Your parents may punish you for the choices you made and you may also be perceived as untrustworthy by them. This is not an example of exercising Self-Serving Strategies because your decision to harbor a runaway was wrong, you may be punished for your actions and your relationship with your parents may suffer.

#7.) You are in the eighth grade and at a family party. You notice your thirteen-year-old cousin sneaking beer and drinking it. He/she asks you to keep the secret and/or join the private party. No adults suspect any wrongdoing. You know that underage drinking is illegal, but you want to protect your cousin. What are your options?

A.) You decide to keep your cousin's secret, but do not join the underage drinking party. Instead you enjoy the family gathering and ignore your cousin's drinking. He/she gets really drunk and begins to display peculiar behavior in front of the adults. At first, they think it was an act or a joke and then realized that he/she was intoxicated. Because your cousin's symptoms were severe to warrant medical attention, he/she was rushed to the hospital emergency room. He/she was diagnosed with alcohol poisoning, which can be life-threatening. Your cousin stayed in the hospital overnight and then went home and fully recovered in a few days. Your auntie and uncle later asked everyone if they had any knowledge of the underage drinking that was going on at the party. You are very scared to tell the truth, so you deny knowing anything and your cousin backs up your story.
Consequence: You stayed true to yourself by not drinking any alcohol, but you were irresponsible in your decision to keep your cousin's secret. Alcohol poisoning can definitely become fatal if medical attention is not rendered in a timely manner. Although

you did not want your cousin to get angry with you, the best possible choice would always be to tell an adult, especially when illegal activity is taking place. Fortunately, the adults in this situation noticed the symptoms of drinking and the warning signs that followed, which prompted immediate action. You also lied to cover-up your involvement in this incident, which means you will need to continue to lie until eventually the truth surfaces. Believe me it almost always does and at that time you may have other consequences to deal with. This is not an example of using Self-Serving Strategies correctly because your decision to keep this secret may have been fatally harmful to another person. Please continue to read other examples, which may provide you with the tools to effectively use this concept in future dilemmas and situations you may encounter.

B.) You decide the best thing you should do is to be responsible, so you tell your auntie that your cousin had been drinking. Your auntie finds your cousin and notices just how intoxicated he/she is and allows him/her to drink coffee to sober up. Your auntie thanks you for doing the right thing, but your cousin is angry with you for telling. They leave the family gathering and go home.
Benefit: You were very responsible in your decision to tell, although you knew it would upset your cousin. Sometimes doing the right thing causes angry reactions in the people involved because they want to continue doing the wrong thing. This is a great example of building leadership skills, which may benefit your future educational and career goals in a positive manner. Congratulations on effectively displaying Self-Serving Strategies.

C.) You decide to cooperate with your cousin by keeping the secret and joining the underage drinking party. You were curious about how it feels to get drunk, so you drink alcohol until you experience the affects. You get drunk to the point you can hardly walk and everything seems to be extremely funny to you. You are finally able to leave the party with your family and go home. Your parents never knew you were drunk, they just thought you were clowning around and having a good time. The next day you did not feel good, so you convinced your parents that you had the flu and rested all day. After you felt better, you begin to remember how much you liked drinking alcohol and getting drunk. You find ways of getting alcohol and drink whenever it is possible. You like it and want to continue drinking as long as you can, but you do not think you are an alcoholic.

Consequence: Your decision to join the underage drinking party may have caused you to become an addict from curiosity. Discovering just how much you like drinking alcohol may have long-term affects for you and your future goals. Alcoholism is a disease that may take a person an entire lifetime to manage; however, as with any disease, management cannot take place until he/she acknowledges and accepts the diagnosis to be true. Please consider discussing your experiences with a school counselor, your parents, or an adult you can trust to get an assessment. "Addiction Wise" in Chapter #1: The Wise Segments gives suggestions on ways to curb curiosity in a healthy manner and provides ways to learn how to develop healthy solutions for painful experiences. Please review that chapter for clarity, as well as, Chapter #9: The Six Bonus Fundamentals. This is not an example of using Self-Serving Strategies because your decision to drink was not only illegal, but the experience may have caused you to develop an addiction to alcohol. Please seek help.

#8.) You are in the eighth grade and have a stepfather who has developed an inappropriate relationship with you. He gets very jealous of the time you spend with your friends and he taught you the secret touch game. You are very uncomfortable with him, but are scared to tell your mother because she seems to be very happy. What are your options?

A.) You decide to keep this unhealthy, inappropriate relationship you have with your stepfather a secret because you don't want to be responsible for your mother's unhappiness if you tell. You learn to block out the unpleasantness and sacrifice your dignity for the sake of your mom's happiness. You have convinced yourself that she wouldn't believe you anyway, so it really doesn't matter if you tell.

Consequence: Your decision to accept being sexually abused by your stepfather in an effort to keep your mom happy may become detrimental to you and your future.

Bonus Fundamental #1 in Chapter #9:
The Six Bonus Fundamentals states the following:

If you have ever experienced any type of unwanted sexual misconduct, the most important first step is to tell someone. If the first person you tell doesn't believe you, tell another. Tell anyone until someone really hears what you are saying. Only after your testimony has been validated by an adult can you begin the healing process. This violation you have experienced, for whatever length of time, may have long term psychological impediments for you. Proper counseling and treatment will be beneficial for you, especially if explored in a timely manner. Your full potential about who you are and what you will become may have been altered by sexual abuse. This is why coming forward at the onset of ANY MISCONDUCT is critical in the overall healing process. Remember, you are the product of your environment, but your experience does not have to equal to the sum of your life. You can change your future by healing from your circumstantial past, which is the best thing you can do for yourself; thus, displaying Self-Serving Strategies.

It's imperative for you take the above suggested advice to help guide you to recovery. Please remember that you do not have the responsibility to ensure your mother's happiness in any given situation. She is an adult with life experiences and is solely responsible for herself. You do not deserve to live in an unsafe environment that includes ongoing sexual misconduct. This is not an example of using Self-Serving Strategies because your decision may have long term affects for you that may hinder your future goals, and you compromised your best self-interest.

B.) You decide to fight back yourself. You take matters into your own hands. You begin to manipulate and blackmail your stepfather. You threaten to tell your mother in exchange for money and gifts to keep quiet. He becomes agitated with your attitude, so he gives you what you want to keep your mouth shut. You think that you created a win-win situation for everyone because you get extra money and gifts, your mom remains happy, and your stepfather gets what he wants without getting caught.

Consequence: You basically sold yourself and compromised your dignity for money, gifts, and your mom's happiness. You may begin to really like the comforts of having extra money and decide to do other degrading illegal things to keep the cash flowing. Blackmail is in itself a crime and since you think you have created such a great situation for everyone, you may resort to riskier unlawful behavior in the future. You may develop serious psychological problems that may not be detected because you think your arrangement is okay. Your stepfather may become very angry with you and physically abuse you.

Bonus Fundamental #1 in Chapter #9:
The Six Bonus Fundamentals states the following:

If you have ever experienced any type of unwanted sexual misconduct, the most important first step is to tell someone. If the first person you tell doesn't believe you, tell another. Tell anyone until someone really hears what you are saying. Only after your testimony has been validated by an adult can you begin the healing process. This violation you have experienced, for whatever length of time, may have long term psychological impediments for you. Proper counseling and treatment will be beneficial for you, especially if explored in a timely manner. Your full potential about who you are and what you will become may have been altered by sexual abuse. This is why coming forward at the onset of ANY MISCONDUCT is critical in the overall healing process. Remember, you are the product of your environment, but your experience does not have to equal the sum of your life. You can change your future by healing from your circumstantial past, which is the best thing you can do for yourself; thus, displaying Self-Serving Strategies.

Please consider seeking professional help to restore your self-confidence, self-esteem, and self-worth in an effort to heal from these sexually abusive experiences. Please remember that you do not have the responsibility to ensure your mother's happiness in any given situation. She is an adult with life experiences and is solely responsible for herself. You do not deserve to live in an unsafe environment that includes ongoing sexual misconduct. This is not an example of using Self-Serving Strategies because your decision may have long term affects for you that may hinder your future goals, your best self-interest was compromised, and you broke the law.

C.) You decide to stand-up for yourself and reveal the secret to your mother. She takes quick action to get him out of the house and you into counseling. Her first priority is to keep you safe and get you the help you need to recover from sexual abuse. You feel relieved and validated for speaking the truth.
Benefit: Your decision to tell your mom the truth about the sexual abuse you were continuously experiencing from your stepfather put your best self-interest first. Recovering from sexual abuse may take some time, but by taking the first steps, as described in Bonus Fundamental #1 of Chapter #9: The Six Bonus Fundamentals, you have begun your journey for healing and self-discovery. Congratulations on an excellent example of using Self-Serving Strategies efficiently in this very sensitive situation. You also acquired the power of self-definition by taking charge of your life and what happens to it.

#9.) You are in the eighth grade and have vowed to never try illegal drugs. You and some friends are camping in a tent pitched in the backyard of a friend's house. You feel very safe and are having a great time. A couple of friends smoke cigarettes and occasionally ask you to light it for them. You claim not to smoke, but you don't hesitate in lighting cigarettes. On this night, a friend seemed eager for you to light his/her cigarette. You cooperate with ease, but the cigarette kept burning out for some reason. You continue to light it. After quite a few attempts and the presence of profound laughter coming from your friends, you realize that the tobacco in the cigarette was replaced with marijuana! You were smoking weed and didn't even know it. You are very upset with your friend's

69

decision to violate the pact you made with yourself. You have been friends for a long time, but feel disrespected and unsure if you should remain friends. What are your options?

A.) You decide to forgive your friends, after all it was just a prank. You continue your friendship with them. Because you are less trusting of their intentions, you seem to be always watching your back. You feel less connected, but have accepted the change in your relationship because you think it would be devastating if you ended it.

Consequence: You compromised yourself and your beliefs for the sake of remaining friends with people you simply can't trust anymore. You clearly stated that you never wanted to try illegal drugs and that choice was taken away from you. By accepting the actions of your friends as a prank, you allowed them to define who you are; thus not acquiring the power of self-definition. The quality of a friendship shouldn't be measured by its length, but by the level of mutual respect displayed. You did not do what was best for you; therefore this is not an example of practicing Self-Serving Strategies. Please refer to "Friendship Wise" in Chapter #1: The Wise Segments to learn the importance of evaluating current friendships and when to dissolve unhealthy relationships.

B.) You decide to stand-up for your beliefs and remove yourself from the environment immediately. You explain to your friends how upset you are that they took the choice away from you, when they knew about your pact. Your parents pick you up and you honestly explain to them exactly what happened. They are happy that you made the right decision to leave the camp-out. You think about how this incident has affected you, and you realize how their actions also influenced you to light up cigarettes in the first place. Your evaluations resulted in the dissolution of these relationships because they had become unhealthy for you.

Benefit: Your decision to leave and tell your parents the truth was an excellent example of acquiring the power the self-definition. Congratulations! This is a great example of building leadership characteristics invaluable for your future endeavors. Your parents may become more trusting of you and allow you more responsibility and freedom in the near future. Dissolving these friendships because you determined they had become unhealthy for you was a way to proficiently exercise Self-Serving Strategies. Once again, CONGRATULATIONS!

C.) You decide to play along with the prank and smoke the joint like a cigarette. You get stoned and like the relaxed feeling. Your experience with other side effects (munchies, dry mouth, red eyes, etc...) doesn't seem to discourage you from wanting to smoke weed again. After a short time, you hook-up with a drug dealer and buy weed regularly. Although you never wanted to try marijuana or any other illegal drug, you seem happy that you were tricked into trying it because you like it.

Consequence: Your decision to go along with this prank was an example of giving into peer pressure, which may have led you to develop an addictive disease. You also compromised your beliefs and did not recognize the disrespectful, unhealthy friendships you were involved in. Dependency on marijuana may result in a lifelong, agonizing battle for recovery. Although you did not smoke weed for a long time, you may have already developed an addiction to it. *Addiction is not determined by the length of time you engage in the addictive activity, but by whether or not you can stop at any given time. To make this more understandable, just because the person in this example did not smoke weed for years, it does not mean that he/she is not, or can't be, addicted to marijuana. Please refer to "Addiction Wise" in Chapter #1: The Wise Segments for an overview of information and suggestions to develop healthy coping skills. "Friendship Wise" in the same chapter will provide you with the proper definitions and examples of healthy and unhealthy friendships. This is not an example of using Self-Serving Strategies because your decision caused you to compromise your beliefs, give into peer pressure, and may result in a lifelong addiction to marijuana.

#10.) You are in the eighth grade and have a best friend and a boyfriend/girlfriend. One day in school as you were walking to your next class, you caught your best friend kissing your boyfriend/girlfriend. You are instantly shocked, hurt, and angry with what you just witnessed. You want to know why, but don't know if confronting them would be the best way to handle the situation. What are your options?

A.) You decide you want answers and confront them when they are both with you. They try to deny it, but you tell them that you saw them kissing with your own eyes. You ask them why and how they could hurt you this way? Your boyfriend/girlfriend answers your questions very nonchalantly, while your best friend avoids answering you at all. Instead he/she becomes very angry and wants to physically fight with you. An argument breaks out with name calling and profane language used by everyone. You are so hurt and angry that you just don't know what to do next. After yelling and screaming at each other, you decide to leave and go home. You are so hurt and angry that you just don't know how to cope with your emotions. You avoid them in school and refuse to take their calls. Nothing gets resolved and you still don't understand why they did this to you.

Consequence: Your decision to confront them when you were still experiencing raw emotions was probably not the best choice. You may never be satisfied by questioning people who have betrayed your trust and ruined your relationship. Think about it: Does a right answer even exist for a situation like this? You deserve to be mutually respected in the relationships you choose to build. "Friendship Wise" and "Romantic Relationship Wise" in Chapter #1: The Wise Segments provides an overview of healthy and unhealthy relationships. Please consider reviewing this chapter for help on evaluating and dissolving relationships that may have become unhealthy for you. Remember, people who are untrustworthy with you now, will be untrustworthy with you later. Why? Because that's just who they are. This is not an example of using Self-Serving Strategies because your reaction caused an argument that could have included physical violence, which may have injured you and there was no resolution.

B.) You decide to ignore what you saw and pretend that everything is okay with both of these relationships. You carefully observe their behavior and become suspicious of the way they interact with each other. You begin to wonder how long your best friend and boyfriend/girlfriend have been involved secretly. You try to prevent them from having any chance of seeing each other privately by being with your boyfriend/girlfriend constantly. This situation has exhausted a lot of time and energy, which has consumed your life. **Consequence:** Your decision to ignore your boyfriend/girlfriend and your best friend's behavior resulted in you becoming overly cautious of their whereabouts continuously. This is no way to live because you may end up questioning everything and never being satisfied with any answer, since you already know the truth. Your focus may be better served if you concentrated on your personal and educational goals, rather than worrying if your boyfriend/girlfriend is cheating on you with your best friend. Once trust is broken in any relationship, it is very difficult to overcome and repair it. You deserve to be mutually respected in the relationships you choose to build. "Friendship Wise" and "Romantic Relationship Wise" in Chapter #1: The Wise Segments provide an overview of healthy and unhealthy relationships. Please consider reviewing this chapter for help on evaluating and dissolving relationships that may have become unhealthy for you. Remember, people who are untrustworthy with you now, will be untrustworthy with you later. Why? Because that's just who they are. This is not an example of using Self-Serving Strategies because your decision preoccupied you with uncertainty, undue stress, emotional exhaustion, and did not serve your best self-interest.

C.) You decide to walk away and deal with the situation later, when you are calm and the shock is more manageable. You take a few days to ponder a decision. Finally, you realize that having a boyfriend/girlfriend and a best friend whom you simply can't trust is not worth it. The effort it will take to maintain these relationships may consume your life and exhaust your emotional tolerance. You dissolve both relationships separately and privately. Their reactions and/or excuses don't convince you to reconsider your decision. In time, you go on and develop healthy relationships worthy of your commitment and respect.

Benefit: You stayed true to yourself by realizing your own self-worth and by not accepting anything less than what you deserve. Taking some time to really think about the situation and what you were going to do about it was a mature approach and a great example of determining what was in your own best self-interest. Congratulations on a great way to effectively use Self-Serving Strategies.

This completes Chapter #4: The Eighth Grade. I hope the topics presented provided you with an overview of how to use Self-Serving Strategies correctly, effectively, and proficiently. As you practice this concept when dealing with dilemmas, you may become better able to evaluate a situation and make the best possible choice that benefits your future favorably. Learning how to acquire the power of self-definition is an invaluable way of determining your own life's path of triumphs and achievements. I hope you consider taking the advice in Chapter #9: The Six Bonus Fundamentals to help you recognize possible negative influences and experiences that may hinder your future goals. Its purpose is to provide you with unlimited potential by avoiding unwanted memories that may cause flashbacks. Please read on to the ninth grade chapter to preview new examples and challenges you may soon encounter.

Chapter #5
The Ninth Grade

The ninth grade in high school signifies many changes for each and every freshman as he/she enters this exciting time in his/her life. The experiences and memories to be made are that of no other. Interest in romantic relationships may become more prevalent and discovering who you really are may become challenging, but worthwhile, in this first year of high school. Finding your true talent, developing it to the best of your ability, and displaying confidence when performing it, are ways of discovering and displaying true passion. The contemplation of future educational and career endeavors will guide you in creating long-term goals. Most importantly, have fun by getting involved in school activities, events, clubs, sporting venues, etc. Enjoy those special moments... and take PICTURES! You'll thank me later.

Please keep in mind that any and all documented school records, whether it be positive or negative, will remain permanently on those records throughout your entire lifespan. The good news is that if you had a less than favorable past performance record prior to attending high school, you will have a chance at a fresh start. These ten age-appropriate topics are geared to tempt curiosity and to curb risk-taking behaviors that may help you to develop long-lasting life skills that may impact your future in a positive manner. A few examples were created to test your ability to learn how to successfully acquire the power of self-definition. Each example is accompanied by three answer choices and is concluded with a possible benefit or consequence based on that specific option. Please read for clarity and comprehension.

#1.) You are in the ninth grade and at a friend's birthday party. The time has come for the birthday person to open his/her gifts. You watch your friend unwrap very expensive gifts from other guests and begin to feel ashamed of your gift. You really value your friendship with this person, but you don't want to be embarrassed because your gift was inexpensive. What are your options?

A.) You decide to focus on your friendship instead of the price of your gift. You sit proud when he/she opens your gift because you realize that the value of your friendship is not measured by the amount you paid for your gift. Your friend is grateful for your gift and is happy that you were able to attend his/her party.

Benefit: You learned the true meaning of friendship. By being proud and standing behind your gift choice, you displayed a level of confidence that would have filtered out any negative feedback or embarrassment that may have come your way. You begin to develop healthy friendships, as described in "Friendship Wise" of Chapter #1: The Wise Segments. Congratulations on practicing Self-Serving Strategies and acquiring the power of self-definition.

B.) You decide to hide your present and tell your friend that you forgot to bring it. You tell him/her that you will bring it to school the following Monday. The next day you dip into your savings account and go shopping. You purchase a very expensive gift and feel like your friend will like you even more. Your friend opens your gift in school on Monday and doesn't seem to understand why you spent so much money. He/she begins to question you on why? Your friend explains to you that it wouldn't have mattered what the gift was or how much it cost, that what was important was that you were at the party and that your friendship was valued.

Consequence: Because you focused on the price of the gift and not the value of your friendship, you may have compromised yourself. You may not possess the confidence within yourself to know that you are worth being someone's friend, no matter what you give or don't give him/her. Your friend may have gotten offended by your concern over the price of his/her gift and realized that you weren't the friend he/she thought you were. He/she may want to dissolve the friendship with you. Sorry, this is not an example of using Self-Serving Strategies because you displayed characteristics of developing unhealthy friendships by focusing on materialism.

C.) You decide to sit and wait until it is your gift that is being opened. You then start to make excuses for why the gift was cheap. You go on and on about how you did not have enough money to buy the gift you really wanted to purchase for him/her. All the attention was directed at you and people started to talk amongst themselves. When your friend finally gets a word in, he/she tells you that he/she loves the gift just the way it is, cheap or not.

Consequence: You may have embarrassed yourself in front of all the other guests. You may have also made them feel that their gifts were inadequate, too, by emphasizing a dollar amount for your purchase. You may have offended your friend by implying that he/she is a materialistic person who values the price of a gift, rather than the value of the friendship itself. You displayed insecurity when you continued to explain why you bought that gift. Sorry, this is not an example of using Self-Serving Strategies because you displayed characteristics of developing unhealthy friendships by focusing on materialism.

#2.) You are in the ninth grade and have permission from your parents to go out on a group date with a few friends. The plan is to all meet at the designated place and to be picked-up there later by your parents; however, your friends want to make a detour and split the group into couples and spend private time alone with individual dates instead. At the present time, you know you are not allowed to be on a date alone without a chaperone. You like the person that you will be paired-up with, if you decide to cooperate with this dishonest arrangement; however you are not sure if it is worth the risk of losing your parent's trust. What are your options?

A.) You decide to tell your friends that you are not going to deceive your parents with the lying by omission tactic. You explain to them how uncomfortable you are with this deceptive plan and how you are not willing to risk losing your parent's trust. You also decide to tell your parents why you won't be going out on this group date. They are very proud that you decided to make the right choice and thank you for your honesty.

Benefit: You stayed true to yourself by doing what was best for you. Realizing the value of being trustworthy from your parent's point of view and not willing to compromise the current relationship you have with them, is an example of building leadership characteristics.

You also did not give in to peer pressure. All are fine illustrations of using Self-Serving Strategies effectively. You definitely acquired the power of self-definition in this example.

B.) You decide to go and the evening gets off to a great start. You really enjoyed your one-on-one date with this person. You know that you must return by the specified time in order to avoid getting busted;   however, your parents come early to pick you up and you get caught walking as a couple (holding hands with close body language) into the place where you did not have permission to leave. Your parents asked you a lot of questions about where you have been and who that other person was. You decide to tell them the truth, since you quickly realize that lying would be too hard to continuously cover up. Your parents are very disappointed in the choices you made to deceive them.

Consequence: You have broken the trusting relationship you once had with your parents and it may take you awhile to regain it. You may also be punished in some way. You exhibited characteristics of becoming a follower in this situation because you went along with the plan, although you knew that it was wrong and dishonest; thus giving into peer pressure. You did not in any way display Self-Serving Strategies because your choice required you to be deceitful, which hurt your parents. It was not in your best interest to be perceived as untrustworthy by your parents. Please read other examples that may provide you with clarity on just how using Self-Serving Strategies effectively and efficiently can produce desired, positive results for the betterment of your future.

C.) You decide to go and the evening gets off to a great start. You really enjoyed your one-on-one date with this person. You know that you must return by the specified time in order to avoid getting busted. You arrive at the place early and are able to meet with the whole group to discuss any possible questioning from parents. You want to get all your stories straight. Your parents pick you up and only ask you if you had a good time. You answer "yes" and thank them for allowing you to go. A few days go by and the person you had the private date with calls your house and leaves a detailed message about your secret date. Unbeknownst to your parents, this information is welcomed with curiosity and shock. Your parents relay the message to you and your defense is that you did not technically lie because a group of your friends did meet and were picked-up at the designated place. Your justification is that you were never asked if you left the area or were alone with only one person at anytime. Your parents have a serious discussion with you and explain what lying by omission means and how it has created an uncomfortable disconnection in your relationship with them. They are deeply disappointed in your choices and actions that followed.

Consequence: Your decision may have caused you to continuously lie to cover up your secret date, if he/she did not call your house and leave that detailed message with your parents. Understanding what lying by omission is and how it is never successfully used to justify one's actions, may provide you with valuable knowledge the next time you are tempted to defy your parents. It may take a while to regain your parent's trust and you may also be punished in some way. Please grasp the concept of Self-Serving Strategies with a desire to use it in upcoming situations that involve peer pressure in the decision making process for the betterment of your future.

#3.) You are in the ninth grade and feel very isolated and alienated by your classmates. You don't fit in any group and you don't have any real good friends, but you have tried to connect with some students. You really want to develop healthy, genuine friendships, without surrendering to peer pressure, but don't know how. What are your options?

A.) You decide to accept your lonely existence, so you stop trying to develop friendships. You begin to feel isolated and experience symptoms (lack of energy, loss of appetite, sleep more, irrational thinking, anxiety or nervousness, etc.) of depression. You ignore the signs and continue to do nothing to help yourself. You begin to feel as though life is not worth living because you don't feel as though you belong anywhere. You contemplate suicide.

Consequence: Your choice to accept being lonely was very counterproductive. You may have developed depression, or symptoms of depression, by allowing your negative thought process to convince you that you were unworthy of building friendships. Your mind is very powerful and contemplating suicide is a sign of how serious your condition may become. Wanting to end your pain by taking your own life is not the answer to cure your problems. Seeking help from an adult, is the first step to recovery. Sometimes just talking to someone may help. You really need to know that you are worth living a full, productive life. Retraining your thinking patterns to focus on positive affirmations may   help you to build self-esteem and self-confidence. You may need to be evaluated by a doctor to determine if you are indeed clinical depressed. There are different levels of depression, but it is definitely considered a serious illness. With a proper treatment plan, people can recover and live happy, productive lifestyles. Sorry, this is not an example of using Self-Serving Strategies, since your decision has hurt you as a result. Please get help!

B.) You decide to stop trying so hard to establish friendships with classmates; however you do remain cordial with them. Instead, you seek connections with people outside of school that share special interests with you. After a few attempts, you meet a group of young people that fits this description.   Over time, friendships develop and you begin to feel a sense of belonging.

Benefit: You took action for yourself and created an attainable solution that best suited your needs, without hurting anyone in the process. By remaining friendly with your classmates, although you did not feel included with them, you showed maturity and humility. This is a great example of building leadership skills that are admirable now and may become most useful in your future. Congratulations on using Self-Serving Strategies proficiently.

C.) You decide to accept an invitation to join a group of people that continuously break the rules. You know that the things they do are wrong, but you desperately want to belong somewhere. You follow their path of dishonesty and destruction and begin to get into a lot of trouble. You are being labeled as a bad student by participating with this group. You feel you belong, but you know they are not good, genuine friends you can trust to build healthy relationships with.

Consequence: You were not being true to yourself when you made this decision. You placed yourself in direct association with a group of students that you knew engaged in rule-breaking behavior for the thrill of it. This may have negative repercussions for you in your future, especially if the risk-taking behavior continues to increase to meet the level of excitement desired. Although you felt included and a sense of belonging, you compromised your goal of trying to establish healthy friendships without surrendering to peer pressure. This choice also showed characteristics of becoming a follower, instead of the more favorable leader role. This is not an example of using Self-Serving Strategies because you compromised yourself for the sake of overcoming loneliness, which may hurt you in the future. Please disassociate yourself from this group and begin developing positive friendships with people outside of school you may share common interest with.

#4.) You are in the ninth grade and have a friend who has asked you to lend him/her some money. You are not sure when and if you will get your money back, but you feel as though you can trust this person to keep his/her word to repay the loan. You have the money and lending it won't cause you any financial hardship, but you are concerned about ruining the friendship. What are your options?

A.) You decide to lend the money to your friend. He/she promises to repay the loan within two weeks. In the next few days you watched him/her buy frivolous items and you begin to wonder how he/she can afford to buy unnecessary merchandise, but not repay your loan in a timelier manner. You confront him/her and his/her advice to you was to relax. Since the two weeks weren't up yet, the loan is not technically considered late, is the attitude your friend has chosen to take; however, you feel disrespected and used. Eventually you get your money back, but you feel your relationship is tarnished.

Consequence: You may never be able to fully trust this friend again based on the way he/she treated you in this situation. It is perfectly okay to say "no" to a friend, especially if you have doubts. Listen to your heart, but let your mind and thought process guide you in making difficult decisions that may result in a negative outcome. Personally, I have made a conscious choice to no longer lend any money to anyone (friends, relatives, strangers, partners, etc.) because I have experienced first-hand how it can ruin an otherwise healthy, trusting relationship. By practicing Self-Serving Strategies, you may begin to learn how to make decisions that may benefit your future, which may minimize the development of negative experiences and memories for you.

B.) You decide to decline your friend's request to borrow money. You briefly explain to him/her just how much you value your friendship. Because you don't want anything, especially money, coming between your relationship you are not willing to take the risk. Your friend gets a loan from someone else and your friendship remains intact.

Benefit: You stayed true to yourself by realizing the friendship was more important to you than taking the risk of losing it; thus ultimately doing what was best for you. Loaning money to anyone may cause awkwardness for both people involved, so avoiding it altogether may be a good idea. Congratulations on practicing Self-Serving Strategies.

C.) You decide to give your friend the money he/she needs as a goodwill gesture, since it will not be a financial burden for you. You explain to him/her that you gave this money freely from your heart, with no expectations or commitment of repayment. He/she thanks you for your help.

Benefit: You handled this situation in a healthy manner because you gave your friend the money with no obligations or ultimatums attached. This is an example of the universal law of give and take as described in Bonus Fundamental #6 of Chapter #9: The Six Bonus Fundamentals. Basically, what you give out, you will receive; therefore, you may be rewarded for your kindness in a different manner that benefits you. Congratulations on taking a mature approach in your decision. Please continue to use Self-Serving Strategies efficiently.

#5.) You are in the ninth grade and just had your wisdom teeth pulled. You are in a lot of pain, so your doctor has prescribed a pain reliever that contains codeine. You follow the directions on the prescription and the pain subsides. After a few days of taking this medication, you begin to feel better and are almost completely healed. Since you are no longer in any pain, you stop taking the drug . You still have pills left and are tempted to take one because you like the carefree, relaxed feeling the side effects give you. The prescription clearly states that the medication is to be used as directed for pain. The warning sign on the label cautioned that dependency of the drug may lead to addiction. You want to feel calm with no worries on your mind, but you don't want to become addicted to pain pills. What are your options?

A.) You decide to take another pill to get that calm, relaxed feeling back. You continue to take this pill daily, until all the medication is gone. The day that you don't have a pill to take becomes nearly unbearable to handle. You notice how nervous you are and how focused you are on how to get more pills. You have convinced yourself that you need these pills in order to function. You are feeling very desperate and are willing to do anything to get your hands on more pills.

Consequence: Your choice may put you in a very dangerous predicament that may include illegal activity, since you are desperate for this drug. You may be diagnosed with having an addiction to pain pills that may take you a lifetime to curb and/or manage. This decision may also lead you to experiment with illegal street drugs to get the desired effect. Please refer to "Addiction Wise" in Chapter #1: The Wise Segments to learn how addiction may be harmful for you now and in your future. Although your situation involved prescription drugs and not illegal street drugs, the warning label clearly stated the possibility of becoming dependent. Dependency often leads to addiction. This is definitely not an example of using

Self-Serving Strategies because you not only hurt yourself by possibly acquiring an addiction, your decision may also hurt family members and others close to you. Not to mention your future plans and goals. Please seek help as soon as possible.

B.) You decide to give the left over pills to one of your parents. You explain to him/her that you are tempted to take them because you like the side effects you experienced. He/she has a discussion with you about how important it is to recognize behavior that may escalate into serious consequences for you. Your parent also gives you suggestions for natural relaxation techniques that you may use if you are feeling stressed and overwhelmed. You try a few of them and have found a particular technique that works best for you. You are very grateful for learning a healthy alternative to dealing with personal challenges and struggles.

Benefit: Your decision to express honestly what you were feeling regarding the prescription drugs with one of your parents was a mature approach that he/she may have appreciated. He/she may consider you to be more trustworthy since you were very honest in your discussion with him/her. Being receptive to his/her suggestions about how to relax in a healthy manner may have shown him/her that you are open-minded and responsible. You have also begun to build leadership characteristics with this choice. Learning how to take care of yourself and knowing when to seek help are invaluable life skills to attain. This is an excellent example of practicing Self-Serving Strategies efficiently and acquiring the power of self-definition. Congratulations!

C.) You decide to take a pill and you continue to take one daily until the pill bottle is empty. The next day you decide to try marijuana because you learned in health class that one of the side effects was getting a really relaxed, calming feeling after smoking the drug. You begin to smoke weed everyday to recapture that same relaxed, carefree feeling. You are still able to handle your responsibilities (school, homework, chores, etc.) adequately, so you don't see a problem with your decision. In fact, you think you have come up with a great way to handle life's stressors, without any consequences.

84

Consequence: Your decision may have led you to become dependent on an illegal drug, marijuana, in order to deal with life's challenges. This choice may have severe ramifications for you because if that drug no longer satisfies your needs, you may resort to other illicit drugs that may be much more powerful and dangerous. Dependency on any drug (prescription or illegal) is a definite precursor to addiction. Please refer to "Addiction Wise" in Chapter #1: The Wise Segments for helpful information and suggestions on the topic. You may not think you are doing anything wrong or that you are not suffering right now, but if this behavior continues to escalate it may become detrimental to your future. You cannot live your life by not learning how to deal with stress in a healthy, constructive way. You may need to seek professional help from a counselor or enter a rehabilitation program to get back on track. This is not an example of using Self-Serving Strategies because your decision was illegal and it may cause you to become a drug addict, which will never benefit your future in a positive manner.

#6.) You are in the ninth grade and are shopping with some friends in a nearby mall. One of your friends suggests that you steal the items you want from the store because he/she feels they are too expensive to purchase. The group decides to shoplift and needs to know if you are in or out. You really want the things you selected, but you know that stealing is illegal, with severe consequences if you are caught and you are also afraid of going against the group consensus for fear of retaliation. What are your options?

A.) You decide to join the group and steal the items. Everything goes as planned, until you attempt to leave the store. As soon as all of you stepped outside the door, the security guards surround the exits and inform all of you that you've been caught shoplifting and the proof is on videotape. You are all taken to the security office where the police are called. The police arrive and take all of you to the police station where all your parents are called. Since you are all under the age of eighteen and this was the first offense for everyone, you are all released to your parents. The silence in the car ride home is nearly unbearable. Your parents discuss the incident in detail with you and express just how disappointed they are with the choices you made. You are punished accordingly.

Consequence: You did not stay true to yourself. You knew that stealing was wrong; however, you gave into peer pressure by going along with the group's decision. This is an example of becoming a follower, which is not a favorable characteristic to acquire. Your punishment may include the loss of privileges and the cancellation of upcoming events that may have been memorable for you (playing/watching sports, dance, date, etc...). Although you were released to your parents and you don't have a criminal record, this experience did create a negative memory for you. Please refer to Chapter #9: The Six Bonus Fundamentals to learn about being aware of the consequences your actions may create. Making a choice to prevent the retaliation from this group of friends if you did not agree with their plan is not an example of using Self-Serving Strategies correctly. You may think that your choice was in your best interest because you did not need to deal with any teasing or alienation, but you did hurt yourself and commit a crime in the process. These choices you made will definitely not benefit your future positively. Please read on to fully understand the concept and how to use it correctly in future situations.

B.) You decide to just say "NO!" to the temptation of stealing the merchandise. You tell your friends that you are going home now, before they steal anything, because you don't want to be associated in any way with committing a crime. You go home and think very carefully about how your friends have changed their value and belief systems. You decide to limit your involvement with them, until you are no longer considered part of the group. You begin to form friendships with trustworthy people.

Benefit: You not only stayed true to yourself, you also made a difficult decision to discontinue your friendship slowly with this group, which eliminated confrontation and awkwardness, which was in your best interest. This is an excellent example of using Self-Serving Strategies proficiently. Congratulations on acquiring the power of self-definition.

C.) You decide to just say "NO!" to the temptation of stealing the merchandise. You tell your friends that you will wait for them by the exit, but that you will not in any way participate in this crime to be committed. They steal the items and find you at the exit. You all walk out of the store together. You are all quickly stopped by the security guard and are told to return to the store because you were ALL caught shoplifting. In the security office you were all shown a videotape of your actions. You tell the security guard that you did not steal ANYTHING and that the video proves it. He/she informs you that your body language and by positioning yourself at the exit, gave the impression that you were the "look-out" person. Walking out with them also made you guilty by association. The police were called and arrived to take all of you to the police station where all your parents were called. Since you are all under the age of eighteen and this was the first offense for everyone, you are all released to your parents. In the car ride home you explain to your parents that it was not your intention to get involved at all. Your parents discuss the incident in detail with you and express just how disappointed they are with the choices you made. You are punished accordingly.

Consequence: You may have thought you were staying true to yourself by not agreeing to participate; however, you did not remove yourself completely from the situation in a timely manner. Therefore, this is not an example of using Self-Serving Strategies correctly. Guilt by association may encounter the same level of reprimand that a person who committed the crime firsthand may receive. Waiting for your friends to commit a crime should be a crime in itself because you knew it was going to happen and did nothing to prevent it. Your punishment may include the loss of privileges and the cancellation of upcoming events that may have been memorable for you (playing/watching sports, dance, date, etc.). Although you were released to your parents and you don't have a criminal record, this experience did create a negative memory for you. Please refer to Chapter #9: The Six Bonus Fundamentals to learn about being aware of the consequences your actions may create. You may think that your choice was in your best interest because you did not steal anything, but you did hurt yourself and commit a crime in the process. These choices you made will definitely not benefit your future positively. Please read on to fully understand the concept of using Self-Serving Strategies correctly in future situations.

#7.) You are in the ninth grade and have developed feelings for a boy/girl in your homeroom class. He/she does not act as though the feelings are mutual. You want to know how he/she feels about you, but you don't want to be embarrassed. What are your options?

A.) You decide to take a chance and you ask him/her out on a group date. You explain to him/her that you are only allowed to group date at this time. He/she accepts the invitation to join a group of your friends on a fun evening out. During the date you discover that you have a lot in common and realize that you want to pursue getting to know him/her further. At the end of the date, you asked if he/she would be interested in seeing you again. His/her response is "yes" and you continue dating. Over time, and with the "talk" described in the "Romantic Relationship Wise" section of Chapter #1: The Wise Segments, you both agree to engage in a committed romantic relationship.

Benefit: Your choice prompted you to explore the possibility of getting involved with this person. By being engaged in conversation and being perceptive to his/her ideas and beliefs, you realized that you share many common interests. You may have raised your confidence level by asking him/her out without hesitation of the outcome. Following the suggestions in the "Romantic Relationship" section of Chapter #1: The Wise Segments, by having the "talk," you were able to define your relationship and your commitment with each other in a healthy manner. Congratulations on a very fine example of using Self-Serving Strategies effectively and acquiring the power of self-definition.

B.) You decide to take a chance and you ask him/her out on a group date. You explain to him/her that you are only allowed to group date at this time. He/she accepts the invitation to join a group of your friends on a fun evening out. During the date you discover that you don't have much in common. Your values are very different and you are not willing to compromise your belief system for him/her. You discuss your concerns with him/her and you both decide to remain friends. You still have a great time on the date.

Benefit: Your choice prompted you to explore the possibility of getting involved with this person; however, after realizing that you were too different to develop a boyfriend/girlfriend relationship, you both agreed to be friends. This was a mature approach in handling what could have been an awkward situation. You also stayed true to yourself by your unwillingness to compromise your values and beliefs for the sake of a boy/girl you like. Your experience may have taught you that being physically attracted and having emotional feelings for someone is not always enough to develop a healthy relationship. This is why dating with the intensions of getting to know someone and finding common interests plays an important role in the experience, as described in the "Dating Wise" section in Chapter #1: The Wise Segments. This is an excellent example of practicing Self-Serving Strategies proficiently and acquiring the power of self-definition. Congratulations!

C.) You decide not to take the risk of rejection and/or embarrassment, so you don't ask him/her out. You keep your feelings a secret. You go on with your daily responsibilities; however, you think about him/her quite frequently.

Consequence: Your choice may keep you wondering "what could have been?" You may also never know if he/she shared the same feelings for you. A risk is not worth taking if it may involve bodily harm or severe consequences for you, such as the risk of experiencing with illegal drugs. The worst case scenario in this situation was the possibility of being rejected; however, being rejected a time or two also builds life skills by learning how to deal with not getting what you want. As for the risk of embarrassment, if this happened, the best way to overcome it would be to use humor to recover. Although you thought you did what was best for you and you may think that you used Self-Serving Strategies by avoiding a possibly awkward/uncomfortable situation, this choice actually added confusion of the unknown to your thinking process. Next time please take a chance. You may be either pleasantly surprised with the outcome or you may learn a valuable life lesson.

#8.) You are in the ninth grade and have a parent who drinks too much alcohol. His/Her moods are unpredictable and most of the time you live in fear of the unexpected. You don't like his/her behavior and the way you suffer from his/her choice to drink daily. You love this parent, but don't know how to protect yourself without hurting him/her. What are your options?

A.) You decide to seek help from your school counselor. You express your deep rooted feelings and concerns for your safety and future. He/she contacts the proper authorities and your family receives the help that is needed to gain functionality. At first your alcoholic parent resents you, but over time he/she learns to forgive you as part of the overall healing process. You begin individual counseling with a psychologist to start the healing process for yourself. Life seems promising and worth while again.
Benefit: You took responsibility for yourself in this very difficult situation by seeking help, which is an example of using Self-Serving Strategies effectively for the betterment of your future. This choice also gave you the opportunity to acquire the power of self-definition by knowing exactly what you did not want for yourself, then becoming proactive about it. Growing-up in a dysfunctional household is very challenging and the experience may break your spirit and ambition to become the best you can be. Although you are the product of your environment, your experience does not have to equal the sum of your life. Please continue with your counseling, as it will guide you to learn more about acquiring the power of self-definition. Congratulations on taking care of yourself.

B.) You decide to avoid this parent as much as possible. You start to feel the emotional pain and anxiety resulting from your dysfunctional environment. You don't like the discomfort and want to dull the pain, so you begin drinking alcohol. You like how getting drunk numbs the pain and the carefree attitude it brings on. You feel as though you don't have any problems and that all is right in the world when you are drunk.

Consequence: Your choice to numb your pain and stress may result in a life-long addiction to alcohol. This behavior may also give you the desire to experience with street drugs, if you begin to feel drinking is not enough to dull your pain. This choice may become a very serious life-changing addiction for you, which needs to be addressed promptly and properly. Please refer to "Addiction Wise" in Chapter #1: The Wise Segments for suggestions on learning how to develop healthy solutions to pain. Dealing with the main source of your pain by confronting issues and experiences that are attributed to it are the first steps in the healing process. Please get the help you need. This is not an example of using Self-Serving Strategies because you may have developed an addiction for alcohol and/or illegal drugs detrimental for your future.

C.) You decide to take care of yourself and make plans for your future. You make a pact with yourself to never drink alcohol because you have witnessed firsthand how it can destroy your life and family. You continue to do your best in school and have aspirations of attending college. You do not seek any help from anyone because you feel as though you have your life and plans under control. A few years go by and you begin to notice an elevated level of anger that disburses when you least expect it. You don't understand why you react to certain situations in this manner. After all, you took care of your home situation by not letting your alcoholic parent influence your judgment.

Consequence: You may think this is an example of practicing Self-Serving Strategies since you felt you did what was best for you, but this decision eventually hurt you in your future; therefore, it is not. Making plans for your future and pledging an alcohol free lifestyle are steps that were taken in the right direction; however, not recognizing the pain and anger instilled in you from your dysfunctional household has caused an unpredictable chain reaction of anger. These are common symptoms and behaviors that are associated with abusive experiences. Seeking help from

91

a reputable psychologist or equivalent counselor may provide you with understanding and guidance. You still must heal from your circumstantial past in order to live a positive, productive lifestyle with promise and hope. Remember, you are the product of your environment, but your experience does not have to equal to the sum of your life. Please get the help you need.

#9.) You are in the ninth grade and have been teased and harassed by a classmate over a prolonged period of time. Most recently, he/she has created a hate petition for other students to sign. Many students joined the bandwagon of his/her hate campaign against you and signed this document. The students involved have also begun to tease and harass you at their own will. You feel degraded and it has become very difficult for you to attend school. You want these people to leave you alone, but you don't want to be labeled a tattle tale for reporting it. What are your options?

A.) You decide that it would be best for you to take the teasing and harassment, instead of reporting it to a counselor or to the vice principal. You dread everyday of school and often feel nervous walking in the halls alone. Your mind is constantly thinking about what these students might do next. You have a difficult time concentrating in class and your grades have dropped. You are definitely not happy. Living miserably has not been easy to handle.

Consequence: Your decision not to inform anyone of your extreme discomfort these students have caused you may curtail your own education because of your inability to concentrate and stay focused. If your grades continue to drop, your chances of attending the college of your choice may also decrease; therefore, this choice may also affect your future educational plans and goals. Learning how and when to stand-up for yourself in a diplomatic manner may enable you to use Self-Serving Strategies for the betterment of your future. Disclosing your uncomfortable experiences and expressing your feelings to a counselor or to the vice principal is a mature way of advocating for yourself. *Note: You have the right to feel comfortable and safe in school and there are specific laws designed to protect each and every student from such occurrences. The federal mandate Chapter 19 rules clearly outline offenses and the consequences that may be enforced if violated. You can get a copy at any public school in the United States. Private schools have their own set of policies and procedures unique to their campus environment that they follow. No student should suffer needlessly in a school setting.

B.) You decide to confront these students yourself and end up in a heated argument that turns violent. One person takes the leader role of the group and starts hitting you. A security guard notices the fight and breaks it up. You are all sent to the vice principal's office to be reprimanded. Since you started the altercation by confronting the situation in an angry manner, you are just as responsible for the outcome as the person that hit you; however, because there is a zero tolerance law mandated in Chapter 19 for any type of physical violence, the person gets arrested. Your offense is listed under disorderly conduct of the Chapter 19 rules and your consequence is handled by the vice principal.

Consequence: Your choice may have caused you to receive a permanent violation of a Chapter 19 rule on your school record. This may hinder college admissions to your chosen school in the future. You may be suspended from school, or be assigned to mandatory detention. As a result of being hit, you may have been seriously hurt that may or may not require medical attention. You may think you practiced using Self-Serving Strategies correctly because you may view your actions as standing up for yourself; however, your decision did not keep you safe and it may influence your future goals in a negative manner. Please continue to read examples that depict the proper way of using Self-Serving Strategies for the betterment of your future.

C.) You decide to express your discomfort with your school counselor and he/she takes a proactive approach to your situation. The student who started the petition is called into the vice-principal's office and is notified of his/her violation of a Chapter 19 rule pertaining to harassment. He/she is dealt with accordingly. All the students that signed the petition are reprimanded and versed on Chapter 19 rules and the consequences for offenses. You begin to feel protected and are able to attend school in a non-threatening environment.

Benefit: Your decision to inform a counselor of the discomfort you were experiencing from a group of students was an appropriate way to take care of yourself. It is not always easy to put yourself and your needs first, but when done with the intention of resolving a problem and not by trying to get other people in trouble, you begin to advocate for your self. You may now continue your education with confidence and hope for your future plans and goals. Everyone learned how important it is to abide by the Chapter 19 rules, which is mandated by the federal government for all public schools. Congratulations on practicing Self-Serving Strategies for the betterment of your future and acquiring the power of self-definition.

#10.) You are in the ninth grade and have a friend who has disclosed to you his/her deepest secret of bringing an explosive weapon to school. He/she did not give you details about what he/she plans on doing or when it may happen. You don't know if he/she is joking or if this is a serious threat to human life; however, from your observations he/she does seem to be frustrated and angry lately. You don't want anyone to get hurt, but you are not sure of his/her intentions. What are your options?

A.) You decide to take your friend's secret confession as a joke and don't worry about it. A few days go by and you notice your friend carrying a big black bag on campus. You are curious as to what he/she is up to; however, you don't ask any questions. You go to class and don't think twice about it. Near the end of the class period there is a school wide announcement over the intercom alerting faculty and students to remain in their classrooms until otherwise notified. Two hours later you are all released from the buildings and sent home. As you are leaving school campus, you see your friend being escorted into a police car with handcuffs. You then realize the severity of the school wide lock-down. Your friend was caught with weapons in his/her bag, but would not surrender them to the principal. He/she threatened to use a weapon in the office if anyone approached him/her in an attempt to recover the bag. The police and other authorities were called in to deal with this crisis. Eventually he/she surrendered and was arrested.

Consequence: Your choice to ignore your friend's secret may have proved to be deadly, if no one took action to search his/her bag after observing suspicious behavior. If you can't clearly determine if a person's statement is delivered in a jokingly or serious manner, then the best choice is to always report it. These comments should never go unnoticed or uninvestigated. Even if it was meant for a joke, this person probably has deep rooted anger and/or psychological issues that need to be addressed. It is always better to be safe, than sorry. This is not an example of using Self-Serving Strategies because you did not put your safety and the safety of others, first.

B.) You decide to take action by reporting what you know to the school counselor. He/she first investigates the situations to determine the level of danger that may be involved. Your friend is called to the office for questioning and he/she discloses his/her recent hateful feelings for a few students. The school follows proper protocol and a serious crime is averted. Your friend receives the help he/she needs to deal with anger and temperament. Everyone remains safe.

Benefit: You chose to take your friend's comments about bringing dangerous weapons to school seriously and it was the right thing to do. Your friend may be upset with you for telling, but it is always better to ensure the safety of innocent human lives. Reporting it was your civic responsibility because you had the knowledge of a possible crime that could have been disastrous and deadly. This is a great example of using Self-Serving Strategies because you did what was right for everyone, which included yourself.

C.) You decide to question your friend extensively about his/her intentions. He/she does not give you any viable information, so you keep close tabs on him/her. You watch carefully exactly what he/she is doing when on school campus. You continue to do this for weeks and it has begun to deplete your energy. Nothing happens and you feel drained and not focused on your own daily responsibilities.

Consequence: Your decision to spy on your friend in order to ensure everyone's safety may not have been the best choice for you. It is not your responsibility to take charge of a situation that may or may not happen because you "might" know something; however, it is your civic responsibility to report any information that may become dangerous and/or life-threatening to the school counselor, vice principal, or principal. You exhausted all your energy and put your needs last, which is definitely not an example of practicing Self-Serving Strategies. Please understand that taking care of yourself and your needs are an important aspect of achieving your future goals.

This completes Chapter #5: The Ninth Grade. I hope the topics chosen in these examples provided you with a practical approach of how to use Self-Serving Strategies correctly, effectively, and proficiently. It may take practice and a commitment to understand the concept presented, before utilizing it to adequately benefit your future. Please read the upcoming chapters to give you better insight on other subject matters that you may encounter. Chapter #9: The Six Bonus Fundamentals provides an overview of unsolicited advice designed to help you live efficiently by limiting unwanted negative memories and experiences that may hinder your future goals.

Chapter #6
The Tenth Grade

The tenth grade may provide you with a more comfortable environment, since you are now familiar with your surroundings and may have a clearer picture of expectations. By successfully completing the ninth grade, you probably experienced new challenges and predicaments that may have given you the opportunity to learn how to acquire the power of self-definition. If you made some unfavorable choices and accepted the consequences for those decisions, you still have time to redeem yourself. Regrouping and refocusing on defining just who you are and discovering hidden talents and passions you currently possess may help you to create concrete goals for your future. At this age it may be a good idea to build a more trusting relationship with your parents. Balancing school and homework, sports or other activities, personal friendships and romantic relationships, and family responsibilities/obligations (chores, etc.) may be challenging at times, but well worth the effort. Try to stay on track by avoiding negative influences that may deter your path. Remember making time for yourself to relax, rejuvenate, and replenish is very important to your overall success and achievement of goals. Most importantly, have FUN!

The ten topics for this chapter were chosen to provide a variety of specific examples that a tenth grader may encounter. Some situations give the opportunity of how to acquire the power of self-definition, while others are focused on ways to deter peer-pressure. Each illustrated example is followed by three different answer choices and is concluded with a possible benefit or consequence based on the option chosen; however, example answer #10-B includes a benefit and a consequence due to the actions taken after the choice was initially made. Please read with an open-mind and compassion, as some teenagers actually have experienced, or are currently experiencing, some of these real-life encounters.

#1.) You are in the tenth grade, a female and don't like your body size. You compare yourself to other teenage girls your age and you want to look just like them. You think that if you are perceived as being skinny, then you may also be perceived as being popular. You want to feel important and look good, but are not sure how to achieve this. What are your options?

A.) You decide to go on a drastic diet you read about in a magazine. You lose weight rapidly and you like the wonderful comments you receive. People are telling you how skinny you look and you love it. After a few more days, you start to feel weak and light-headed until you faint in class. When you regain consciousness, a classmate helps you to the health room. The nurse asks you a series of questions to probe why you fainted. The subject of eating disorders was mentioned and you deny having a problem with eating. You explain to the nurse that you have been following a dieting plan and exercise regiment regularly, but that you don't have the symptoms of anorexia or bulimia. You just wanted to look skinny because you did not like your body size and you wanted to look like other girls your age. The nurse gives you detailed information about the diseases and explains to you that your current way of thinking may be the beginning stages of developing an eating disorder. You are referred to a counselor for help with body image and self-acceptance.

Consequence: You may have begun to develop the beginning stages of an eating disorder. Your decision to lose weight was not to become healthier; it was to try to become popular. Most, if not all, fad diets are unhealthy. If you want to lose weight for the right reasons (better health, training, etc.), then following a healthy eating pattern and an exercise regiment regularly may provide you with your desired result over time. Quick weight lose is never healthy, nor does it last. Counseling may help you to accept yourself for the wonderful person you are now, despite the size of your jeans. This is not an example of using Self-Serving Strategies because your decision was made for the wrong reasons and done in an unhealthy manner, which was not in your best interest. Please try to understand that who you are as a person has nothing to do with how much you weigh or the size of your clothes.

B.) You decide to talk to an adult about how you are feeling. He/she tells you that the pressure you are experiencing to be skinny and perfect may be coming from outside influences that may be affecting you negatively. For example, the media's portrayal of a beautiful woman may require her to be a perfect size 2 and if she is full bodied, then she may be perceived as being chubby or overweight. Depending on how a young woman feels about herself first may determine her interpretation of these media images. The adult also explains to you the importance of raising your self-worth and self-confidence to reach the level of self-acceptance. You consider his/her advice and insights and do some deep searching within you. After careful self-evaluation, you realize the only reason you want to be skinny is to be popular. You contemplate your choices and decide to love yourself for who you are now.

Benefit: Your decision to express your feelings with an adult whom you trust was a great way to gain valuable information. Learning how to self-evaluate and really think about what motivates your actions and exactly why you want something are very valuable skills to attain. In this example, a shift in your attitude and perception instantaneously raised your self-worth. Counseling may help you to reach the self-acceptance level. Congratulations on your decision to seek the advice from an adult, which was in your best interest. Thus, practicing Self-Serving Strategies effectively and acquiring the power of self-definition.

C.) You decide to stop and observe the students on school campus. You realize that people come in all different shapes and sizes. You watch this chubby girl (your opinion) and you notice how happy she looks and acts. You wonder why her weight does not bother her. Why doesn't she want to look like other girls? You ponder the reasons for her positive attitude and can't seem to understand her great disposition. You decide to privately ask a school counselor how a chubby girl could possibly be happy with herself. The counselor explains to you that if she is comfortable with herself just the way she is and she is not intimidated by or envious of skinny girls, then she probably has mastered self-acceptance. The counselor also tells you that a person's level of self-worth and self-confidence determines how he/she feels about himself/herself. This girl shows signs of self-acceptance by being happy and comfortable with herself. The counselor asks you some tough questions about how you feel about yourself and you respond honestly. You begin to really hear yourself talk and realize that your self-worth and self-confidence levels may need improvement. You ask for help and receive it. With hard work, you have learned how to accept yourself for who you are now. You no longer want to be like someone else for the sake of popularity.

Benefit: Your decision to observe another student's behavior and attitude before taking any action to try to become skinny was a mature approach. Asking a counselor his/her opinion on the subject gave you valuable information and insight about how important self-worth and self-confidence is in determining your perception of yourself. After realizing that you may need to improve on the way you feel about yourself, you did the right thing by asking for help. Congratulations on using Self-Serving Strategies in an effective way for the betterment of your future and for acquiring the power of self-definition.

#2.) You are in the tenth grade and love art class. You discovered you have talent in drawing and painting different unique design patterns. A classmate notices your work and invites you to become a tagger with his/her team. He/she explains how great it would be to have your designs and symbols on big public buildings, bridges, and walls. You know that this type of "art work" is really classified as graffiti, which is a form of vandalism and the crime committed would be criminal property damage; however, you think it would be cool if many people could see your creations. You know it is wrong to vandalize, but you crave notoriety. What are your options?

A.) You decide to accept the invitation and you go on the next tagging project, which was to spray paint symbols and designs on a big, concrete wall in a residential neighborhood. Since the plan requires you to meet the group at 11:00 p.m. on a Friday night, you get permission from your parents to sleep-over your new friend's house. You both sneak out of his/her house at 10:30 p.m. that night to meet the tagging team. The wall was located at the entrance of a newly built subdivision. Everyone began creating his/her own unique artistic designs in specified areas of the wall. You were assigned the lower right end of the wall, which was closest to the main road with high visibility. You took the challenge and put your talent to work. At 11:45 p.m. the police arrive, driving from inside the subdivision to surround the group of taggers. The watch person was stunned to see the police there because no sirens were heard and no police cars entered the subdivision. Apparently this neighborhood had recently integrated a community watch program with its last walk through at 11:30 p.m. nightly. People trained to search for criminal behavior in their neighborhood smelt the paint and saw some teenagers climbing the main entrance wall to vandalize it. The police were called and a request was made for a silent approach from the back entrance. You all get caught and take a ride to the police station. Your parents are called to pick you up.

Consequence: You did not stay true to yourself by agreeing to join this tag team because you knew their "artwork" was really graffiti and unlawful. This example exhibited the development of becoming a follower, which is not a favorable characteristic to posses. You may be arrested, which may have severe consequences for your future plans. Your parents may become less trusting of you, since you got caught in a lie about where you were and what you were doing. Learning to listen and trust your inner voice may lead you to better outcomes. This is definitely not an example of using Self-Serving Strategies.

B.) You decide to turn the offer down and seek recognition from other sources. You ask your teacher about possible opportunities to showcase your artwork and he/she informs you of an art contest in the community and the annual school art exhibit. You enter the contest and your artwork is seen by many people, the other contestants, the general public, and the official judges. You feel validated and recognized for your natural talent. You also place your masterpieces in the school art exhibit and you receive positive feedback. You feel good about yourself and proud that you did not resort to illegal temptations in an effort to achieve notoriety.

Benefit: Your decision may have enabled you to learn how to advocate for yourself by inquiring about opportunities that best suits your needs and talents. You stayed true to yourself, displayed confidence, and showed leadership in this very fine example of practicing Self-Serving Strategies and acquiring the power of self-definition. Congratulations!

C.) You decide to accept the invitation and you go on the next tagging project, which was to spray paint symbols and designs on a big, concrete wall in a residential neighborhood. Since the plan requires you to meet the group at 11:00 p.m. on a Friday night, you get permission from your parents to sleep-over your new friend's house. You both sneak out of his/her house at 10:30 p.m. that night to meet the tagging team. The wall was located at the entrance of a newly built subdivision. Everyone began creating his/her own unique artistic designs in specified areas of the wall. You were assigned the lower right end of the wall, which was closest to the main road with high visibility. You know it is a very risky area, but you took the challenge and put your talent to work. When everyone was done, you leave and go back to your friend's house. You think everything is great because you did not get caught and your creations are on display for people to notice; however, the vandalism was reported on the evening news the next day and the police are going to investigate the few leads they have on the case. The newscast also reported the quick cooperation of the neighborhood in dealing with this crime by painting over the graffiti immediately. You now live in fear of getting caught and your creation was covered-up.

Consequence: You did not stay true to yourself by agreeing to join this tag team because you knew their "artwork" was really graffiti and it is unlawful. This example exhibited the development of becoming a follower, which is not a favorable characteristic to posses. Although you did not get caught at the time of the crime, living in fear of being caught may be more unsettling for you. The outcome of your choice has created a lose-lose situation for you, since you are afraid and did not receive the recognition you craved for your creations. This decision may also lead you to take higher risk-taking challenges and invitations in an effort to feed that hunger for attention. This is not an example of using Self-Serving Strategies because you did not do the right thing and you still may have more consequences to face if you do get caught. It may be wiser to curb that need for attention in a more positive manner.

#3.) You are in the tenth grade and although you try your best in school, your grades don't seem to reflect your efforts. Sometimes you just don't understand or you can't seem to concentrate on your schoolwork and you feel stupid. Your grades are important to you because you plan on going to college. You want to earn better grades, but don't know how to get help. What are your options?

A.) You decide to ask your teacher for help. He/she agrees to tutor you after school. You still experience difficulties learning, so your teacher suggests you get tested for possible learning disabilities that may include medical conditions. You get tested and are diagnosed with a documented learning disability that does not suggest or require medication as a plan of treatment. The best chance for improvement is to define what learning style best suits your chance for success. After your teachers modify and create a learning style that best suits your ability to learn and introduce you to various focus techniques, you improve and begin to gain self-confidence.

Benefit: You asked for help from a teacher, which is a great example of advocating for yourself. Dealing with your frustration by your willingness to create a solution that best suited your needs and promise for your future, is an outstanding exemplification of how to use Self-Serving Strategies proficiently. Congratulations on the commitment you have made for yourself and your future endeavors and for acquiring the power of self-definition.

B.) You decide to talk to your parents about your frustrations in school. They carefully consider your situation and decide to get you tested for different types of learning disabilities. These tests show that you have been diagnosed with an attention-deficit type of disorder that suggests or requires medication as a plan of treatment. Your family discusses the options and risk factors involved with the doctor and they decide to allow you to take the medication on a trial basis. After a few days, you are able to concentrate on your schoolwork and you begin to feel confident in your ability to learn. **Benefit:** You asked for help from your parents and they took your situation seriously and got you the proper help you needed. Being able to openly discuss matters with your parents is an example of having and/or creating a trusting relationship with them. Congratulations on using Self-Serving Strategies to ensure the success of your future educational goals and acquiring the power of self-definition.

C.) You decide to suffer and accept the fact that you are stupid and unable to learn. You continue to go to school and try your best without disclosing your learning challenges or frustrations to anyone. Your parents are disappointed with your grades because they think you are not trying your absolute best in school. Based on your current grade point average, you realize that you will probably have to go to community college. You really planned on attending a university out of state.

Consequence: Your choice to keep your learning challenges a secret may hurt your future plans and goals. By not asking for help to identify the problem to find an explanation for your frustration, you may never discover your true academic potential. Your parents may reprimand you for your low achieving report card, since they were not informed of your difficulties in school. This is not an example of practicing Self-Serving Strategies because your decision may hurt your future plans, goals, and your relationship with your parents. Please consider this: Help is always available for those who ask for it.

#4.) You are in the tenth grade and have friends who have pierced different parts of their bodies. You especially like the tongue and belly button piercings. They have all told you that they did not experience any problems or infections due to their piercings. They have also been able to successfully hide it from their parents. You are contemplating getting a piercing, but are afraid of getting caught and/or getting an infection as a result. What are your options?

A.) You decide to get a belly button ring, since it would be the easiest to hide. A few days after the piercing you noticed swelling, redness, and other signs of an infection in the area. You try to disinfect the wound with peroxide, but the symptoms don't seem to diminish. You begin to get scared and as a last resort, you tell your parents what you did. Your parent's first concern is to deal with your infected wound. You are taken to the doctor and the piercing is removed, the wound is cleaned properly, and you are prescribed antibiotics to be taken for the next ten days. The doctor explains to you that piercing different body parts may not be a good idea because if an infection does occur, as in your case, an open wound may put yourself at risk for serious bacterial diseases. He/she adds that some bacterial infections and diseases may become life-threatening if medical attention is not sought immediately. Your infection begins to heal with medication and frequent cleansing. Your parents then deal with your dishonesty.

Consequence: You could have developed a serious life-threatening medical condition if you did not tell your parents what you did in a timely manner. Your parents may become less trusting of you because you got a piercing without their permission or knowledge and tried to hide it from them; however, it was a good choice to seek help instead of continuing to try to handle it yourself. You knew you had concerns about the possible outcomes, but you still agreed and went along with it anyway. Learning to listen to those doubts and your inner voice may provide you with insight and maturity. The initial choice is not an example of using Self-Serving Strategies because your decision was made in deceit and it may have had severe health concerns for you.

Benefit: You did the best thing for yourself and your health by telling your parents what you did, so that you could get the proper help you needed. Hiding health issues from your parents is never a good idea. No matter what you may have done. Their first priority is and always will be your health and safety. Congratulations on practicing Self-Serving Strategies in the aftermath of your original decision. It is never too late to instill this concept for the betterment of your future, especially when it may concern your health.

B.) You decide to get a belly button ring, since it would be the easiest to hide. After a few days of swelling and redness in the area, it heals properly. You are happy and don't foresee a problem getting caught, since it is in an area that is always covered up; however, one day you felt extremely tired and fell asleep on the couch in the late afternoon. One of your parents came home early from work and noticed a shiny piece of jewelry dangling from your belly button while you were sleeping. He/she quickly woke you up and questioned you about the piercing. You decide to answer honestly. You are told to remove the ring from your belly button and keep it clean until the piercing closes up.

Consequence: You may be punished for your actions. Your parents may become less trusting of you, since you did not seek their permission and tried to deceitfully hide it from them out of fear. This is not an example of using Self-Serving Strategies because your decision required deceitful actions that may also develop into a distrustful relationship between you and your parents. The latter is not in the best interest of your future, as an untrusting parental relationship may hinder your plans and goals.

C.) You decide to ask your parents for their permission to get a belly button ring, which requires a piercing. Both of your parents deny your request and explain the adverse affects of piercing unconventional body parts. After listening to their reasons and understanding the risk factors that may be involved, you decide to pass on the idea. You just don't think it is worth defying your parents and taking the medical risks.

Benefit: You stayed true to yourself by first asking for permission, actively listening to your parents' reasons why and making the right choice for yourself. Your parents may become more trusting of you because you handled this situation with maturity by overcoming temptations to defy them. Congratulations on a great example of using Self-Serving Strategies proficiently.

#5.) You are in the tenth grade and a group of classmates want you to cut class after lunch recess with them. You don't really like your afternoon classes, so you consider going. You know that it is wrong to cut class and you may get caught for truancy from the police. You want to go because you feel daring and you think it would be fun, but you are afraid of getting busted. What are your options?

A.) You decide to cut class after lunch recess and you have a great time dodging the cops and defying school rules. You don't get caught and you return to school the next day. Your parents are not notified of your absences in your afternoon classes. You feel empowered and daring.

Consequence: Your decision, since you did not get caught, may lead you to higher risk-taking behaviors that may result in severe consequences for you and your future. You did not stay true to yourself because you knew it was wrong to cut class, but you allowed temptation to overwhelm your judgment. This may be an indication of becoming a follower, which is an unfavorable characteristic to attain. This is not an example of practicing Self-Serving Strategies because your choice may lead you down a path of dishonest, defiant behavior, which may be detrimental to your future plans and goals. Not getting caught this time is not necessarily an indicator of invincibility. Please make wiser choices for the betterment of your future.

B.) You decide to cut class after lunch recess and you get caught by the police for truancy. You and your culprits are taken to the police station and are reprimanded for breaking the truancy law. Your parents are called to pick you up. Your parents discuss your actions and deal with your daring adventure.

Consequence: You did not stay true to yourself because you knew it is wrong to cut class, but you allowed temptation to overwhelm your judgment. This may be an indication of becoming a follower, which is an unfavorable characteristic to acquire. You may be arrested and you may face disciplinary action from your school's principal or vice-principal under Chapter 19 violations for truancy. Any possible disciplinary action taken will remain on your permanent high school record, which may hinder college admission to your preferred school. Your parents may punish, or take privileges away from you. They may also become less trusting of you, which may hurt the relationship you've built with them thus far. This is not an example of practicing Self-Serving Strategies because your choice may have severe consequences for your future educational goals and your relationship with your parents.

C.) You decide to turn down the offer to cut class because you don't want to take the risk of breaking the truancy aw. Although you don't like your afternoon classes, you realize that attending and making the best of it would be a wiser choice than avoiding it altogether. You are proud of yourself for making the right decision.
Benefit: You stayed true to yourself by making the best possible choice for yourself and your future goals. By turning down the offer to cut class, you exercised leadership skills that may develop into building great characteristics that may influence your future positively. Learning how to make the best of a class requirement you don't particularly care for and not giving in to peer pressure, showed maturity. Congratulations on using Self-Serving Strategies effectively for the betterment of your future.

#6.) You are in the tenth grade and have been invited to a party on Saturday night by a group of people you don't know that well. They inform you that if you decide to go, you will need to bring some alcohol with you; however, they do not suggest stealing it from your parents. Instead they have devised a plan that has worked in the past that will require you to stand in front of a liquor store and ask someone to purchase some beer for you, until someone agrees to buy it. You know that underage drinking and purchasing alcohol for minors are illegal, but you are curious and adventurous. You are tempted to go to the party because you have never tasted alcohol before, but are afraid of the risk factors involved. What are your options?

A.) You decide that you really want to go to the party and are willing to take the risk of getting and bringing alcohol. You ride your bike to a liquor store in another neighborhood where you are less likely to run into people you may know. You wait in the parking lot for someone who looks cool; someone you think will buy beer for you. After an hour or so, a young man pulls into the parking lot. You ask him and he agrees to buy you beer. You give him the money and he returns with a 12-pack of beer. You put it in your backpack, get on your bike, and begin to leave the parking lot. The young man gets in his car and drives to the exit of the parking lot. You hear sirens and are informed by the police to stop. The young man's car is blocked by a police car at the exit. The police inform both of you that this liquor store has been under surveillance and that your exchange of money and alcohol was recorded on tape. You are both taken to the police station in different squad cars. The young man is arrested for illegally purchasing alcohol for a minor and your parents are called.

Consequence: You let curiosity overshadow your judgment, took a chance, and got caught. You gave into peer pressure by following the plan, although you knew it was wrong and risky. Although you are a minor, you may be arrested and face criminal charges. Your parents may be less trusting of you and you may be punished for the choices you made. Engaging in risk-taking behaviors because you are curious and adventurous may prove to be dangerous for you and your future. "Addiction Wise" in Chapter #1: The Wise Segments explain that an addiction can derive from curiosity and offers suggestions on how to curb that curious nature. Please review that chapter for comprehension. Learning how to use Self-Serving Strategies in peer pressured situations may keep you focused on your future plans.

B.) You decide that going to this party is not worth the risk of getting caught with alcohol. The next day, you decline the offer and a few members of the group begin teasing and calling you a "chicken." You stand-up straight, feel very confident, and respond by simply saying "Bounce." You then turn around and walk away.

Benefit: You did what was best for you, without allowing the teasing and immature behavior to affect you. Knowing what risk-taking behaviors you are not willing to undertake builds character, leadership skills, and a sense of self. Congratulations on a great example of practicing Self-Serving Strategies in this peer-pressured situation. You also acquired the power of self-definition. This example incorporated "Bounce" described in Bonus Fundamental #3 of Chapter #9: The Six Bonus Fundamentals.

C.) You decide that you really want to go to the party and are willing to take the risk of getting and bringing alcohol. You ride your bike to a liquor store in another neighborhood where you are less likely to run into people you may know. You wait in the parking lot for someone who looks cool; someone you think will buy beer for you. After an hour or so, a young man pulls into the parking lot. You ask him and he agrees to buy you beer. You give him the money and he returns with a 12-pack of beer. You put it in your backpack, get on your bike, and leave to go to the party. The young man gets in his car and drives away. You arrive at the party and give the beer to the group. They give you one beer and tell you to leave the party. Since you supplied them with the alcohol, they no longer needed you. They used you to take the risk, but will not reward you by allowing you to stay. You go home feeling awful.

Consequence: You gave into peer pressure by doing exactly what was asked of you; although you knew it was wrong. You decided to trust a group of people whom you knew engaged in illegal activity and then you were surprised when they turned on you. Learning to observe character traits in the people you choose to hang-out with may provide you with insight of how they will treat you in future encounters. Chapter#1: The Wise Segments explains the importance of establishing healthy friendships in "Friendship Wise," and illustrates that a person may become an addict by curiosity in "Addiction Wise." These segments also offer suggestions on how to curb your curiosity and evaluate your friendship realm. Please review this chapter for clarity and comprehension. This is not an example of using Self-Serving Strategies because your choice caused you to get your feelings hurt, your curiosity for drinking may result in alcohol dependency, and it was illegal!

#7.) You are in the tenth grade and consider yourself to be a good friend; you treat your friends with respect and loyalty. Lately you have noticed that one of your friends is not mutually respecting you or your friendship. He/she hasn't returned your phone calls in a timely manner and always seems to have an excuse not to hang-out with you. Recently you have heard from others that this person is talking very negatively about you behind your back. You don't understand what happened to your friendship with him/her. You want to know why this person is treating you unfairly, but you are not sure how to approach the situation without getting hurt or rejected. What are your options?

A.) You decide not to take any chances of getting hurt or being rejected by accepting the change in your friend's attitude with you. He/she continues to follow a non-reciprocal friendship pattern. Although you don't like feeling unimportant and unworthy of respect from this person, you tolerate it out of fear. You think that, over time, he/she will come to realize the value of your friendship and start to treat you better.

Consequence: Your choice may cause you to experience emotional distress that may last longer than recovering from hurtful feelings or being rejected. You made a decision to continue with an unhealthy relationship that compromised your self-worth, self-esteem, and self-respect; therefore, this was not an example of using Self-Serving Strategies correctly. Please refer to "Friendship Wise" in Chapter #1: The Wise Segments for suggestions on establishing healthy friendships and learning when to break unhealthy relationships. *You are worth having good, healthy friendships now; therefore, waiting for someone else to realize your value empowers him/her to define who you are. One of the main goals of using Self-Serving Strategies for the betterment of your future is to acquire the power of self-definition. This basically means that you have the power within yourself to define who YOU are, without being influenced by others. With practice and perseverance, you too can achieve this level of empowerment.

B.) You decide to ask him/her if there is a problem with your friendship because you have noticed a significant change in his/her attitude. After a calm, rational conversation with him/her you learn that his/her behavior was triggered by a misunderstanding. Apparently, he/she overheard you talking to someone and misinterpreted the language used and thought that you no longer wanted to be friends with him/her. You receive an apology from him/her and he/she wants your relationship to go back to how it was; however, you know that his/her actions displayed disrespect and immaturity, clear signs of an unhealthy friendship pattern. After careful thought and evaluation, you decide that it is in your best interest to dissolve this friendship. You don't think you can trust him/her anymore because of the way he/she chose to handle the situation. You know how important open communication is in any and all relationships and you won't settle for anything less than what you deserve. You remain polite and cordial when you see him/her.

Benefit: Your decision to calmly ask him/her directly if there was a problem with your friendship was an example of effective communication. Learning the reasons for his/her behavior, then analyzing future encounters with him/her, gave you insight into doing what was best for you. Your mature approach and focus on yourself is a great example of practicing Self-Serving Strategies for the betterment of your future and acquiring the power of self-definition. Congratulations!

C.) You decide that two can play the same game and start talking bad about him/her to other classmates. Your goal is to hurt him/her before you get hurt again. This hurtful name calling game continues to be played by both of you for a few days. Nothing gets resolved and you both get your feelings hurt. It finally ends when he/she unexpectedly punches you in the face. You fight back because you have a lot of built-up anger and pain. Now, you are both physically hurt and still nothing has been resolved. You leave and go home. You avoid him/her as much as you can.

Consequence: You decided to play the same game and still ended up getting your feelings hurt. You also got physically hurt. The old saying "two wrongs don't make a right" is a true statement. Your goal was to hurt the other person for personal gain, which is not an example of using Self-Serving Strategies as defined in the introduction of this book. You may think you were protecting yourself by choosing this plan of action but intentionally hurting someone else will almost always result in hurting yourself too (as illustrated in this example). You may never know why your friend was treating you disrespectfully because you did not ask him/her. Please take a proactive approach in dealing with similar situations in the future that include effective communication.

#8.) You are in the tenth grade and have never tried any type of illegal drug. A friend of a friend has asked you to try some marijuana after school. You are tempted to try it because you don't see any harm in smoking it just once. You don't think you will become dependent on it because it is an herb, so there should be no problem. You are feeling stressed and this person has told you it will help you to relax. You know that smoking marijuana is illegal, but you are still tempted to try it just this once for relaxation purposes. What are your options?

A.) You decide to accept the offer, after convincing yourself that it will be just this once and that nothing bad will happen. You meet your friend's friend after school as planned and you smoke a joint with him/her. You begin to feel relaxed and calm. Your problems and worries seem to be inconsequential. You liked your experience and want to smoke weed again, so the next day in school you ask this person if you could buy a joint from him/her and over time he/she becomes your drug dealer. You can't fathom the possibility that you may have developed an addiction to marijuana. All you know is that you like feeling the effects and you don't think you will survive without smoking weed because you don't know how to deal with life's stressors sober. You keep smoking weed by using all of your money to support your habit.

Consequence: This is an example of becoming an addict from curiosity, as defined in "Addiction Wise" in Chapter #1: The Wise Segments. Recovering from any addictive disease takes time, hard work, and a true commitment for healing to be successful. This "one hit of a joint" decision may have taken a negative detour in your future goals. By shifting your focus on getting "high," instead of planning and achieving your educational goals, you may have placed undue stress and unnecessary harm to yourself. When your money resources are depleted, you might resort to drastic measures to get cash. Please consider seeking professional help immediately. *Addiction is not determined by the length of time you engage in the addictive activity, but by whether or not you can stop at any given time. To make this more understandable, just because the person in this example did not smoke weed for years, it does not mean that he/she is not, or can't be, addicted to marijuana. This is not an example of using Self-Serving Strategies because your decision resulted in the development of an addictive disease, which may have serious consequences for you and your future goals. Please review "Addiction Wise" in Chapter #1: The Wise Segments for alternative suggestions on how to curb your curiosity in a positive manner. You may also learn healthy solutions to pain and coping skills, if you smoke weed to numb yourself from emotional experiences, in the same chapter.

B.) You decide to turn the offer down after weighing all the possible consequences that may result. After school you meet your friend's friend and when he/she asks you if you want to try smoking a joint, you simply say "no, thank you" take a step back, turn around, and walk away. You don't give him/her an explanation, nor do you deliver your statement rudely. You continue to walk home with a great sense of empowerment. You begin to evaluate the friendships you currently have to determine if they are healthy or unhealthy.
Benefit: Your decision to decline the offer to try weed for the first time was an example of not giving into peer pressure. Your actions enabled you to acquire the power of self-definition. Considering whether or not your friends still share your value system is a mature approach to deciding who you want to associate with. You have taken a great step in developing leadership skills and trustworthy characteristics, which are both very favorable attributes.
Congratulations on demonstrating Self-Serving Strategies for the

betterment of your future. Note*: This answer choice was taken directly from Bonus Fundamental #2 in Chapter #9: The Six Bonus Fundamentals.

C.) You decide to turn the offer down, after weighing all the possible consequences that may result. After school you meet your friend's friend and when he/she asks you if you want to try smoking a joint, you say "NO WAY!" with an angry tone. You go on to call him/her awful names and pass judgment for his/her involvement with drugs. He/she is not happy with your response and the only way he/she knows how to defend himself/herself is through physical violence, so a fight breaks-out. You are hit numerous times, until you are able to get away.

Consequence: Your decision to say "no" to the offer to try weed was great, but your hostile approach was unnecessary and proved to be dangerous for you. Confronting a person whom you know engages in illegal drug activity is never a good idea. He/she may display unpredictable behavior because he/she may have trigger points that ignite anger, as in this case. You may have experienced a better outcome if you followed the suggestion in Bonus Fundamental #2 of Chapter #9: The Six Bonus Fundamentals. This is not an example of using Self-Serving Strategies because, while the choice to decline the offer was the right one, your judgmental attitude caused you to experience physical violence. Please consider the source before you decide to voice your convictions. Always remember to place yourself in a safe environment for your own protection.

#9.) You are in the tenth grade and like a boy/girl in one of your classes. You finally got the nerve to ask him/her out on a date and he/she turned you down. You feel like a fool for asking and never want to ask another boy/girl out again. You think rejection is too painful and embarrassing to deal with, so you don't want to risk getting hurt again. What are your options?

A.) You decide to go back and ask him/her why you were turned-down for a date. He/she explains to you the reason (it does matter what the reason is) and you quickly regain your confidence.

You realize that it is not you he/she is rejecting, but rather the opportunity to get to know you better. You decide you will ask someone else out for a date in the near future.

Benefit: You openly asked why he/she did not want to go out with you, which is an example of effective communication. The reason helped you to realize you were not being personally rejected. This is an example of using Self-Serving Strategies because you needed clarification and you asked for it, which was in your best self-interest; however, if your self-esteem was at a higher level, you may not have needed to ask for an explanation. You allowed this person to self-define who you are by giving him/her the power to explain, when it really shouldn't matter to you. Stand tall and accept the fact that you are worth it right now.

B.) You decide to use this let-down as a learning experience, so you don't allow it to influence your decision to ask someone else out in the near future.

Benefit: You didn't ask why you were turned-down because your self-esteem is determined by how you feel about yourself, and not how others may feel about you. Congratulations on acquiring the power of self-definition and exercising Self-Serving Strategies efficiently.

C.) You decide that you don't want to take the risk of being rejected, so you never ask anyone out again. You just don't think you can handle getting hurt or being embarrassed another time. You remove any romantic thoughts about dating guys/girls from your mind and you focus only on school and your future goals.

Consequence: Your decision was solely based on fear, which may compromise growing pain experiences. Teenage dating is part of growing-up and developing social skills. By eliminating it from your life, you may lack experience in building relationships and communicating your feelings effectively. Focusing on school and your goals are great, but not if it is all you are doing. You still need balance in your life and a chance to have some fun. Everyone has experienced rejection before; however, the only way you will ever know how great it feels to hear a "yes" answer is to keep asking until it happens. And it will. I promise. Sorry, this is not an example of using Self-Serving Strategies because your decision may have hurt future dating possibilities and great experiences for you.

#10.) You are in the tenth grade and are being raised by a single parent who takes illegal drugs almost daily. You have witnessed him/her smoke methamphetamine or ice, cocaine, and marijuana with his/her drug friends. There never seems to be enough money for food and basic necessities. His/her moods are unpredictable and most of the time you live in fear of the unexpected. You love this parent; however you don't like the bad choices he/she continues to make. You want to live in a drug-free, safe environment, but you don't want to hurt your parent. What are your options?

A.) You feel hopeless with your situation and decide to disclose your family secret to a school counselor. He/she immediately notifies the authorities and you are placed in a foster home. You feel awful for turning your parent in, but are more relieved that your living situation has been improved. Your parent is very mad at you because he/she MUST now take responsibility for his/her own actions. Basically, the party is over. You feel anxious, confused, and second guess your decision to come forward. With proper, continuous counseling and guidance you learn how to overcome your guilty feelings and realize that you did the right thing for everyone involved. You now live a stable lifestyle and your parent is receiving the help he/she needs.

Benefit: You made a very difficult decision in order to save yourself. This situation, sadly, is one that many children live with across the country on a daily basis. Fear usually limits any action or help they may want to seek and the foreseeable truth is that they become stuck in this vicious cycle of drug abuse and neglect at the hands of their own parents. By taking a stand and realizing that you deserve to live in a safe, drug-free environment, and then taking action for that dream to become reality is a tremendous example of using Self-Serving Strategies effectively, efficiently, and proficiently. This is also a great example of acquiring the power of self-definition. Congratulations and good luck with all your future endeavors.

B.) You decide to confront your parent about his/her drug use and ask him/her to get help. Your parent denies being involved in any drug activity and therefore states that he/she does not need any help. He/she becomes very angry with you for your accusation and verbally and physically abuses you until you are able to get away. You then decide that you've had enough of this crazy, unpredictable lifestyle and ask an adult for help. After a few days of investigating the situation, the authorities officially remove you from the house and you are placed in a foster home. You receive the counseling and help you need to cope with your unfortunate experiences and your parent receives the help he/she needs.

Consequence: Your decision to confront a person whom you know is doing drugs, since you witnessed it firsthand, was probably not a wise choice. Denial is a very common reaction for drug addicted individuals to take. Remember drug abuse deters judgment and reality. You may have been hurt during the angry outburst. You may think you used Self-Serving Strategies by taking matters into your own hands to find a solution, but this is a situation for an adult to handle, not a teenager caught in the middle of the chaos. You are not responsible to fix your parent, but you do have the power within yourself to make choices that may better your lifestyle conditions.

Benefit: You decided during the aftermath of this incident that you had had enough and that it was time to seek help. Although risky and probably very scary for you, this was the best choice you made for yourself and the unlimited possibilities you may now have for your future. This enabled you to get the help you needed to live in a stable, safe environment where YOUR goals and dreams may be realized. Congratulations on using Self-Serving Strategies in the second part of this life-changing occurrence.

C.) You decide not to do anything. You continue to live in a household that does not provide you with the basic necessities for survival; enough food, school supplies, clothing, and emotional support. You avoid this parent as much as possible. Your own dreams and goals for your future seem bleak.

Consequence: You decided to accept your lifestyle condition as is and it may have severe adverse affects for you and your future. You may not get the proper nutrition you need for human growth and development, and this may affect your learning capabilities. You may also become prone to health conditions and diseases in the future. With an upbringing that excludes mutual respect, unconditional love, and emotional support, but includes a drug-addicted parent, the chances of you becoming an addict may dramatically increase. You may think that you will never do drugs because of your experience, but the reality is that it was taught to you by example as a way of coping with life's stressors. If you did not seek help for yourself to heal from these circumstances, then you would not have learned healthy alternatives to dealing with life's challenges and you may resort to using drugs. This is not an example of using Self-Serving Strategies because your decision to avoid the situation and your parent may result in severe consequences now and in your future. Please seek help from an adult you can trust. Life is not easy, but by learning life and coping skills, it can become manageable. I wish you the best in your recovery efforts.

This completes Chapter #6: The Tenth Grade. I hope these topics provided you with an overview of how to use Self-Serving Strategies to make decisions for the betterment of your future. With practice and perseverance, you too can acquire the power of self-definition. Please continue to read Chapter #7: The Eleventh Grade and Chapter #8: The Twelfth Grade, which depicts explicit, in depth subject matters that include life-changing consequences that you may encounter. Chapter #9: The Six Bonus Fundamentals may help you to avoid unwanted negative flashbacks or limitations that may deter your future goals.

Chapter #7
The Eleventh Grade

This chapter is devoted to all eleventh grade juniors in high school. This school year may be filled with excitement, evaluation, triumphs, challenges, and determination. Choice of college; whether to stay home or attend a school out of state, deciding on a major/career, obtaining a driver's license, balancing work and school, learning how to deal with the complexities of romantic, interpersonal relationships, conforming to your own individuality, and avoiding peer pressure are all prevalent for teenagers of your age.

This chapter provides ten examples of specific topics that you may experience as a junior. Each preview is followed by three different answer choices and each answer choice has either a consequence or a benefit added as a possible result; however, example #3-A contains a consequence and a benefit based on the original choice made. Example #7-A, B & C has both a consequence and a benefit listed as possible outcomes due to the life-changing subject matter. Please read for understanding and comprehension.

#1.) You are in the eleventh grade and work in a fast-food establishment. You become very irritated with the behavior of one of your co-workers. You feel as though you are being treated unfairly because this co-worker comes to work late, doesn't pull his/her weight and chatters with other employees in front of customers. You know this is unacceptable, unprofessional behavior. You decide you've had enough and want to take action, but are not sure how. What are your options?

A.) You decide to quit in the middle of your shift. You punch your time card and walk out the door because you are angry and fed-up with the situation.
Consequence: You are out of a job and have lost your main source of income. You may have earned a less than desirable employment record, which may make it difficult for you to find employment in the future. Your best self-interest will not be served in this

decision; therefore, this is not an example of using Self-Serving Strategies. Removing yourself from an environment that causes you stress is different from running away from a situation that you view as a problem.

B.) You decide to finish your shift and set-up a meeting with the manager. In this meeting you explain your experience with this co-worker and start comparing yourself to him/her. You let your boss know that this person really irritates you.

Consequence: You may be labeled a tattle-tale. Your boss may think you are too sensitive to handle minor social conflicts in the workplace, which may prevent you from the consideration of job promotions. You may have also given your boss the impression that you are perfect, which may lead to the perception of being arrogant. Confidence is an invaluable character trait to possess, but it's something that is within yourself that is projected out and not something you have to convince others you have. This is not an example of using Self-Serving Strategies because your choice may cause you numerous negative inferences in the future.

C.) You decide to continue to perform to the best of your ability. You accept the fact that not every co-worker displays your work ethic. You make a conscious choice and a real effort of not allowing anyone to irritate you, which may possibly affect your job performance.

Benefit: You keep your job. You may be considered for a job promotion later. You may be labeled a team player capable of handling social situations in the workplace by the management. You may receive a favorable recommendation when it is time for you to move on. By providing yourself a win-win outcome, without hurting anyone in the process, you have demonstrated Self-Serving Strategies. You also acquired the power of self-definition. Congratulations!

#2.) You are in the eleventh grade and have your driver's license. You are an excellent student and you have never gotten in any major trouble in or out of school. Your close friends invite you to a party with people you are unfamiliar with and you accept the invitation. You get permission from your parents and you volunteer to be the driver for the evening. You fully understand your curfew is 11:00 p.m. At this party, you realize that these people engage in unlawful activities that you have no experience with. There are alcoholic beverages everywhere. You decide to try a beer or two, just for the experience. Five beers later you realize that it is 10:30 p.m. and you have to drive everyone home, including yourself, within the next thirty minutes. You begin to feel dizzy, but you still think you are able to drive safely. What are your options?

A.) You decide to drive everyone home. You get everyone home safely and get in your house just in the knick of time to meet your curfew. Your parents are still up and ask how your evening went? They notice a slur in your speech and suspect that you've been drinking. After a few denials, you confess to drinking at the party. Your parents are very disappointed at the fact that you decided to drive after drinking alcohol. They become horrified with the possibility of what could have happened to you and your passengers in your car and innocent drivers and/or pedestrians you may have come in contact with.

Consequence: You could have killed yourself or others by trying to prove that you could drive while being intoxicated. You also could have injured yourself and others very seriously in a car accident. You displayed no respect for human life, which is precious and irreplaceable. Because you got everyone home safely this time does not signify a guarantee that you will be that lucky if you decide to "chance it" again. Please, please remove the dare devil mentality from your mind and don't do this again - no matter how old you are. This is definitely not an example of using Self-Serving Strategies because of the potentially dangerous choices you made underage drinking and drunk driving.

B.) You decide to call your parents at home and explain the situation. Your mother and father arrive at the party to pick you, your friends, and your car up. Everyone gets home safe and sound. Your parents are a little disappointed with you because you drank alcohol at this party, but they are more relieved that you made the right decision in calling them for help.

Consequence: You chose to drink alcohol when you know it is illegal because you are underage. Although this was your first time drinking, you still may develop an addiction for alcohol. Please refer to "Addiction Wise" in Chapter #1: The Wise Segments for guidance and information relating to addictive diseases. This is not an example of using Self-Serving Strategies.

Benefit: Your second choice, after realizing you were drunk and not able to drive, ensured the safety of everyone involved. By doing what was right, you displayed maturity and your parents may become more trusting of you in the future (but they may still be concerned about you drinking). A great example of practicing Self-Serving Strategies after a wrong, initial choice was made. Please remember "It is always better to be safe, than sorry."

C.) You decide to let another person drive your car. This person has had experience drinking and had less to drink this evening, so he/she should be able to handle driving everyone home safely. Everyone gets in the car and soon realizes that this person drives like he/she is on a race track. You begin to get very nervous and ask this person to stop, but it is too late. He/she hits a telephone pole, after misjudging a left turn.

Consequence: Someone may have been killed or seriously injured in this car accident. Your decision was made very ignorantly because it is never okay to drink and drive, no matter what the amount of alcohol intake is. There are other factors involved that determine how a person may react to drinking alcohol. Stress level, fatigue, body weight and mental stability, just to name a few. Everyone is different and comparing yourself with the five beers you drank to a person that has had less to drink that night, but more experience is not an accurate assessment because both are incompatible. It is really NEVER okay to drink and drive! NEVER!!! This is not an example of displaying Self-Serving Strategies, even though you realized that you couldn't drive while being intoxicated, you passed the responsibility of driving onto another person who was also drinking, which has proven to be just as dangerous and could have affected the lives and futures of many people.

#3.) You are in the eleventh grade and on school campus. One of your friends has handed you a soda can that is filled halfway with hard liquor, with the remaining half containing soda. He/she tells you that it is called a mixed drink and offers you a sip. Lunch recess has just begun, so you have another thirty minutes until you have to report to your next class. You don't want your friend to think you are a "chicken" for not wanting to try it, but you are afraid and time is not on your side. What are your options?

A.) You decide to take a little sip and begin to choke because you were not expecting the strong taste. You go to the nearest restroom to rinse your mouth out. A campus security guard noticed how you rushed to the bathroom and decided to investigate. He/she asks if you needed help. You answer "No." The security guard smelled the alcohol on your breath and you are quickly escorted to the principal's office. After your parents arrive to join the meeting, you learn that your school has a strict policy on underage drinking on campus. You make a conscious choice to tell the truth, which meant telling the principal exactly who gave you the drink in the first place. Those students were called in later to be reprimanded.
Consequence: Depending on your school's policy, disciplinary action may include suspension or expulsion. Chapter 19 rules will be enforced, so you may be arrested by the police for underage drinking. This incident and disciplinary action will remain on your permanent high school record indefinitely; therefore, college acceptance may become more challenging. This is definitely not an example of practicing Self-Serving Strategies.
Benefit: When you decided to tell the complete truth, which meant giving your friends up, you displayed Self-Serving Strategies because you did what was best for you. Although your decision has caused your friends to be reprimanded, it was the right thing to do. The principal needed all the information to discover the source of the offense to address the problem as a whole. This

is not an example of infringing on another person's rights or causing a person to experience hurtful feelings, as described in the introduction of this book.

B.) You decide to decline the offer by simply saying "No, thank you." Then you take a step back, turn around and walk away. You do not give an explanation or an excuse and your actions did not display any rudeness.
Benefit: By taking these two important steps, you have empowered yourself by displaying an excellent example of practicing Self-Serving Strategies. Congratulations!!! You also acquired the power of self-definition. *Note: This illustration was taken from Bonus Fundamental #2 in Chapter #9: The Six Bonus Fundamentals.

C.) You decide to take a sip and discover you like the taste. You ask your friend for more, and when your friend declines your request, you wait until after school to look for alcoholic beverages at home. You find hard liquor in your parent's "off limits" cabinet. You are not sure which hard liquor bottle contains the alcohol you tasted earlier, so you decide to taste them all. You quickly learn that it is not a good idea to mix drinks, as you begin to feel very sick. You are able to hide your "flu like symptoms" from your parents and siblings by going to bed early. The next morning your head hurts, really hurts. You call your friend that introduced you to your first sip and he/she explains that you are experiencing a hang-over. He/she gives you some advice of how to cope with it and then laughs and teases at you. After you recover from your hang-over, you realize that you enjoyed being drunk. You like the feeling of being "high" because it makes all your problems seem so trivial. You keep drinking by using all of your money to support your habit.
Consequence: This is an example of becoming an addict from curiosity, as defined in "Addiction Wise" in Chapter #1: The Wise Segments. Recovering from any addictive disease takes time, hard work, and a true commitment for healing to be successful. This "one sip" decision may result in s negative detour for your future goals. By shifting your focus on getting "high," instead of planning

and achieving your educational goals, you may have placed undue stress on and unnecessary harm to yourself. When your money resources are depleted, you might resort to drastic measures to get cash. Please consider seeking professional help immediately. *Addiction is not determined by the length of time you engage in the addictive activity, but by whether or not you can stop at any given time. To make this more understandable, just because the person in this example did not drink for years, it does not mean that he/ she is not, or can't be, addicted to alcohol. This is not an example of using Self-Serving Strategies because your decision may have resulted in the development of an addictive disease, which may have serious consequences for you and your future goals. Please review "Addiction Wise" in Chapter #1: The Wise Segments for alternative suggestions on how to curb your curiosity in a positive manner. You may also learn healthy solutions to pain and coping skills, if you drink to numb yourself from emotional experiences, in the same chapter.

#4.) You are in the eleventh grade and you begin scouting for colleges that interest you. Your parents want you to attend any one of the few nearby colleges or universities in your hometown. You aspire to go to a college or university that best suits your needs and the major you are interested in. You don't want to disappoint your parents; however, you do want to fulfill your own dreams. What are your options?

A.) You decide to call a family meeting. During the meeting you express the importance of going to a college or university that best fulfills your educational interests and goals. You go on to explain to your parents that you fully understand how much they will miss you, so you promise to come home during winter and summer breaks. You also make a financial commitment to actively contribute to the additional educational expenses by applying for ALL scholarships you are qualified for and to get a part time job on campus. You demonstrate true passion for the major you have chosen and you believe that you will achieve your educational goals.

Benefit: By providing a presentation that included empathy for your parent's feelings and solutions for the extra financial expenses, you showed just how serious you are about going away to college. This approach also displayed a mature way of using negotiating skills to meet your needs. Whether or not your parents agree to let you attend school out of town, you can be proud of the way you handled the situation by voicing your convictions diplomatically. Congratulations on a great example of practicing Self-Serving Strategies.

B.) You decide to give in to your parents wishes and choose a college near home. You will need to change your major because it is not offered at that school. You will continue to live at home. You are happy that your parents will be happy, but you are not excited about attending college because you do not have true passion for your chosen major, since it's a substitute for what you really want to do.

Consequence: You did not stay true to yourself when you decided to fulfill your parent's wishes and not pursue your own dreams. Although your decision may have prevented hurtful feelings and unwanted emotional distress to develop for your parents, it was not the best choice for you. Curtailing your educational endeavors to save your parents heartache is not an example of displaying Self-Serving Strategies. Creating a plan that includes compromise on both sides may result in a solution that best suits you and your parents. Don't be afraid to ask for what you want, you may be surprised with the answer.

C.) You decide to tell your parents exactly where you will go to school, whether they like it or not. Your demands prompt an unfavorable response from your parents and the discussion ends in a heated argument. Your parents are angry and hurt at the way you TOLD them what your plans are. Your actions created an uncomfortable environment, which made it impossible to resolve the differences between you and your parents; therefore, the final decision has been put on hold.

Consequence: Your decision may have hurt your chances of attending any out of town school because it showed immaturity and disrespect. Your actions may have convinced your parents that you are not ready to take on the responsibility of living far away from home. You may need to regain your parent's trust since your outburst was unwarranted and unnecessary. You may want to convert telling your parents what you are going to do, into asking them what you want to do. Learning and implementing Self-Serving Strategies as a decision-making tool may provide you with better results in future.

#5.) You are in the eleventh grade and have been in a romantic relationship with your boyfriend/girlfriend for nearly one year. You get into a heated argument on school campus with him/her and he/she hits you hard enough across your face that it leaves a very noticeable mark that turns into a bruise. You are shocked and walk away, without saying anything to him/her. You are not sure how to handle this situation, since it is the first time you have ever experienced interpersonal violence. What are your options?

A.) You decide to talk to your boyfriend/girlfriend about the incident a few days later. You explain to him/her that you will not tolerate any abusive behavior. You go on to explain that the relationship is not working for you right now and you want to take a break. During this break, you do some research and discover that other occurrences of behavior that he/she had displayed previously are also considered abusive. You learn that possessiveness and a controlling type of personality were two key factors that contribute to the beginning stages of the cycle of abuse/violence. You also learn that you may have a level of responsibility in this situation because of your tolerance level of being treated inappropriately. You meet again, but this time you have a third person there to witness the planned final break-up and to help keep you safe. Because you are unsure what his/her response will be, you take these added steps to protect yourself.
Benefit: Your decision has empowered you by realizing that your self-worth is high, valuable, and will not be compromised. By doing the research, learning what part you played in this relationship, taking responsibility for your tolerance level, and creating an

exit plan that provided additional protection for yourself, you successfully displayed Self-Serving Strategies. You also acquired the power of self-definition. Congratulations!

B.) You decide to talk to your boyfriend/girlfriend later that day and he/she apologizes profusely for hitting you. He/she goes on to promise that it will NEVER happen again; you cover-up the bruise with make-up and lie to anyone that asks how you got it. Your boyfriend/girlfriend is extra nice to you for the next two weeks, until you decide to disagree with him/her. Because he/she cannot control his/her anger, you get hit again. The violence continues and begins to escalate with intensity and frequency. You find yourself constantly lying to your parents, friends, teachers, counselors, etc. about all the marks and bruises on your body.

Consequence: By giving your boyfriend/girlfriend another chance without fully understanding the severity of his/her violent outbursts, you may have created the current lifestyle choice for yourself that includes repetitious lying and unbearable isolation. Learning to love yourself more than you fear your boyfriend/girlfriend may raise your self-worth and lower your high tolerance level for abuse. Please review "Romantic Relationship Wise" in Chapter #1: The Wise Segments for information on how to distinguish between a healthy and an unhealthy romantic relationship. You have the power within yourself to heal from interpersonal violence, if you believe you are worth saving. Because you tolerated your boyfriend/ girlfriend's behavior, made excuses to cover-up his/her abuse, and compromised your self-worth, you did not use Self-Serving Strategies.

C.) You decide to go and hit him/her back. You begin to have a fist fight, while classmates gather around to watch. The security guard is notified and you both are taken to the principal's office. Because the fight happened on school campus, Chapter #19 rules are enforced. The police are called and you are both arrested. Your parents are called to pick you up from the police station. You are informed by reading the school's official report that you are suspended from school for one week. You are very angry because you feel that this situation was not your fault, since you did not start it.

Consequence: You decided to deal with the situation by reacting with your own anger. Anger vs. Anger never results in an amicable outcome. This decision has caused you to get suspended, which will remain on your school record permanently. Because you are a minor, your arrest record may be voided once you become a legal adult at the age of eighteen. Although you did not start the fight, you definitely contributed to it. Learning how to take responsibility for your own actions and trying to contemplate those actions before you make a choice, are two of the most important steps in practicing Self-Serving Strategies. Please review other examples to give you more insight into how to use this concept correctly.

#6.) You are in the eleventh grade and your best friend of many years has just confided in you that he/she is gay. You are shocked and confused about this very personal secret that he/she has been hiding from everyone. You are not sure what to do or how to react, especially since you are the only person who knows. What are your options?

A.) You decide that the value of your friendship is not based on each other's sexual preference and keep him/her as your best friend. You keep his/her secret and offer support whenever he/she needs it. You feel secure in your relationship in knowing that he/she is not attracted to you; that you are valued only as a true friend. Your friendship has always exhibited a healthy reciprocated friendship pattern with mutual respect and appreciation; therefore, you feel comfortable with your decision.

Benefit: You stayed true to yourself by knowing exactly who you are by evaluating the measurement of your friendship solely based on the relationship that you both have built over the years and not on his/her sexual preference. This displayed maturity beyond your years and respect for yourself and him/her. This is a very fine example of using Self-Serving Strategies. Congratulations!

B.) You decide to tell him/her that you no longer want to be friends because you are heterosexual and not homosexual. You don't want him/her to be attracted to you, so you distance yourself as much as possible from him/her. When other friends and classmates begin talking about and teasing him/her, you become a willing participant.

Consequence: Your choice to dissolve this friendship was not necessarily wrong because you felt uncomfortable keeping it; however, your decision to distance yourself from him/her was based on the assumption that he/she would become attracted to you if you didn't. This is probably an inaccurate notion. You may have allowed fear to control your better judgment. Although you may have felt you made the best possible choice for yourself, your behavior after the fact may have caused your former friend to experience hurtful feelings, thus not displaying Self-Serving Strategies. Learning how to deal with your fears in a constructive manner may provide you with a better outcome.

C.) You decide to dissolve your friendship with him/her because you feel that you no longer have enough in common. You explain exactly how you feel about the whole situation and you promise to keep his/her secret. You end up becoming casual friends with him/her (acknowledgement, making small "talk") when you see each other. No ill willed feelings transpire between the both of you.

Benefit: By analyzing the changes in your relationship that may occur based on your friends sexual preference, you came to the conclusion that you will no longer have enough in common with him/her. This was a very honest and fair evaluation. Although it may have been a painful decision for you to make and him/her to take, no animosity was exchanged between you. Your actions displayed leadership skills, communication skills and mutual respect in a difficult situation. These are all admirable traits to attain and polish for your future. Congratulations on a very fine example of practicing Self-Serving Strategies efficiently.

#7.) You are in the eleventh grade and are a female. You have been sexually active with your boyfriend of two years for the last five months. You have been careful to use birth control properly; however, you have just discovered that you are indeed six weeks pregnant. You don't quite understand how this could have happened, since you felt you were being responsible by using protection each and every time. You are very scared and are not sure just what to do. What are your options?

A.) You decide, after careful consideration, that having an abortion would be the best decision for you at this time in your life. You know that neither your family, nor your boyfriend's family would be able to financially support a baby right now. You told your parents your predicament and they contact a reputable doctor to get the procedure done. You felt adoption would not be the right decision for you.

Benefit: You handled this very difficult decision with maturity and respect. You had enough respect for your parents to inform them of your situation and they supported your choice and took the proper steps to ensure your health and safety. TEENAGERS! PLEASE, ALWAYS TELL YOUR PARENTS!!! There are some states where it is legal for underage young women to go to a clinic to have an abortion WITHOUT PARENTAL PERMISSION! I know sometimes this may be hard to believe, but your parents do really love and care for you. It is their right to know exactly what, if any, medical procedure you may be undergoing, especially when you are still a minor. Congratulations on practicing Self-Serving Strategies in a very difficult and life-changing predicament.

Consequence: You may wonder about this child for the rest of your life. Bonus Fundamental #3 in Chapter #9: The Six Bonus Fundamentals clearly states the possibility of experiencing an unwanted pregnancy, even if you are responsible to use birth control each and every time sexual activity occurs. This is a fact because the only 100% effective birth control that currently exists is total and complete abstinence. It also states that you may never be the same, no matter what your decision is. Please review all six bonus fundamentals at your convenience and for the benefit of your future.

B.) You decide to have the baby and give it up for adoption, after outweighing the three possible choices: abortion, adoption or keeping the baby. You knew that you could not give this child the proper nurturing and financial stability he/she deserves for a great start in this wonderful world. Your parents contact an attorney to deal with the legalities and complexities of adoption. A married, childless couple awaiting a bundle of joy of their own becomes blessed with your healthy baby.

Benefit: Your decision was based on maturity and reality. You knew that you were not ready to care for a baby on a full-time, lifetime basis. Recognizing this at your age displayed maturity beyond your years. You made the new parents of your baby very happy. Congratulations on practicing Self-Serving Strategies in very difficult and life changing predicament.

Consequence: You may wonder about this child for the rest of your life. Bonus Fundamental #3 in Chapter #9: The Six Bonus Fundamentals clearly states the possibly of experiencing an unwanted pregnancy, even if you are responsible to use birth control each and every time sexual activity occurs. This is a fact because the only 100% effective birth control that currently exists is total and complete abstinence. It also states that you may never be the same, no matter what your decision is. Please review all six bonus fundamentals at your convenience and for the benefit of your future.

C.) You decide to have and keep your baby. You thought about adoption; however, you don't want to go through life wondering what ever happened to your son or daughter. You create a support system with your family, boyfriend, close friends, school counselors, and extended family members. You also make concrete plans for the financial responsibility of caring for your baby. You plan on graduating from high school and applying for scholarships and grants to attend college close to home. You have considered all the sacrifices you will be faced with and your decision is final because you already love your baby. You can't bare the thought of living without him/her.

Benefit: You made a decision that best suited you for this particular situation. You also put plans in place to create a favorable outcome, which may reduce the stress level and anxiety associated with first-time motherhood. Your plan to finish high school and continue your education in college may benefit your future tremendously. You will not become the statistical teenage mother; uneducated, irresponsible, with no hope for the future. Congratulations on practicing Self-Serving Strategies in a very difficult and life-changing predicament.

Consequence: You may miss your freedom and easy-going lifestyle you once had as a teenager. You may lose friends and not be able to attend school functions and events because the responsibilities of caring for a baby must come first. Bonus Fundamental #3 in Chapter #9: The Six Bonus Fundamentals clearly states the possibly of experiencing an unwanted pregnancy, even if you are responsible to use birth control each and every time sexual activity occurs. This is a fact because the only 100% effective birth control that currently exists is total and complete abstinence. It also states you may never be the same, no matter what your decision is. Please review all six bonus fundamentals at your convenience for the benefit of your future.

#8.) You are in the eleventh grade and have been in a committed, romantic relationship with your boyfriend/girlfriend for nearly one year. You witnessed first hand him/her cheating on you. You are deeply hurt and are unsure of how to handle the situation. What are your options?

A.) You decide to walk away from the situation to gather your thoughts. Later you discuss the matter with your boyfriend/girlfriend. You calmly explain to him/her exactly what you witnessed. He/she tries to convince you that it was "nothing" and implies that you were seeing things. You trust your own judgment, since you saw them with your own eyes. You quickly realize that he/she not only cheated on you, but also is trying to lie his/her way out of it. You value your self-worth and make the painful decision to end this relationship because it has become unhealthy for you.

Benefit: Although this choice resulted in you experiencing a lot of pain from this break-up, you did what was best for you. Knowing who you are and exercising your zero tolerance level for ANY inappropriate behavior may prevent you from compromising your beliefs and values in future situations. Congratulations on displaying an excellent example of using Self-Serving Strategies in a very difficult and painful situation.

B.) You decide to confront him/her on the spot. Tensions erupt and an argument results in the use of very hurtful language. Your boyfriend/girlfriend tells you that he/she has wanted to break-up with you for sometime now, but did not know just how to do it. You are shocked at learning this information from him/her because you did not think there was anything wrong with your relationship. The other person involved in this confrontation is watching with a big smile on his/her face, as though he/she won the jackpot. The pain you experience is almost unbearable, not knowing what to do next, you react to the situation by yelling and crying hysterically. You just can't believe he/she would do something like this to you. A friend takes you home. The days that follow are filled with anger, pain, and shock.

Consequence: Your decision to confront him/her, while he/she was caught in the act of cheating, was probably not a wise choice. His/her actions required this conversation to be conducted personally and privately. Confrontations can be successfully executed, but the time, place and state of mind of all parties involved have to be considered to reach a favorable outcome. You did not give yourself any time to comprehend what you saw or to think about what you should do next. It is best to approach a situation like this when you are calm, strong, and ready to deal with whatever excuse he/she may try to give you as an explanation. You would be surprised to find out what a difference a day may make. Sorry, this is not an example of using Self-Serving Strategies because you reacted too quickly with anger, before thinking about the situation thoroughly.

C.) You cheat on him/her for revenge. Later, you feel awful for the choice you made. You know that two wrongs don't make a right, but you wanted to get back at him/her for the pain and shock he/she caused you to experience.

Consequence: Your decision has direct negative repercussions for you, whether or not he/she finds out the truth of your unfaithful actions. Instead of dealing with him/her in a mature way, you chose to engage in behavior that displayed a lack of self-respect and self-esteem for yourself. You compromised your beliefs and values by cheating on your boyfriend/girlfriend, when you knew first hand how much it would hurt. Please make choices in the future that benefit you, without hurting anyone else in the process; thus practicing Self-Serving Strategies. It takes time to retrain your mind to adapt to this concept, but your diligence may pay-off when your future begins to show promise and hope.

#9.) You are in the eleventh grade and have been in a committed, romantic relationship for nearly one year. Thus far, you have not engaged in any type of sexual activity and want to remain a virgin until you decide otherwise. Your boyfriend/girlfriend feels it is time to take your relationship to the next level, which includes sexual intercourse and other sexual encounters. You are not ready and have expressed your convictions to him/her; however, he/she continues to pressure you. Your boyfriend/girlfriend believes that if you agree to have sex with him/her it will strengthen your relationship and prove your commitment to him/her. You love him/her, but are not ready to have sex. What are your options?

A.) You decide not to engage in any sexual activity because you feel you are not ready. You discuss your final decision with him/her and he/she realizes just how much pressure you have felt from him/her. An apology follows a lengthy conversation from him/her and you both agree that now is not the time to take this big step in your relationship. He/she accepts the fact that your relationship is already strong because you have the ability to communicate and make decisions together with mutual respect.

Benefit: You communicated successfully to him/her what you are not willing to do to prove your loyalty or the measurement of strength in your relationship. This is an example of understanding and executing Bonus Fundamental #4 in Chapter #9: The Six Bonus Fundamentals. It is also an example of using Self-Serving Strategies proficiently and acquiring the power of self-definition. Congratulations on putting your own needs and wants first.

B.) You decide to have sex with him/her. You did it to make him/her happy by proving your love and showing your commitment to the relationship. You thought that this would strengthen your relationship, but the opposite occurred. Shortly after you gave in to your boyfriend's/girlfriend's sexual desires, he/she broke-up with you. You felt devastated because you shared a very personal, first-time intimate experience with him/her at his/her request, but soon realized that you were used.

Consequence: You compromised your own values and self-respect by having sex with him/her for all the wrong reasons. Please read Bonus Fundamental #4 in Chapter #9: The Six Bonus Fundamentals, which clearly illustrates the difference between sex and love. Although you may be upset about this break-up, you may soon realize that this person's ultimate goal was to just have sex with you; therefore, the dissolution of this relationship was actually in your best interest. Hopefully this experience will have taught you how to be completely true to yourself and how to make decisions that benefit you and your future, thus practicing Self-Serving Strategies.

C.) You decide not to have sex with him/her and he/she gives you an ultimatum; either you have sex or the relationship is over. You continue to refuse his/her request and don't appreciate the threat of your relationship ending because you are not willing to give him/her sex. You then accept the break-up with grace and respect because you know the value of your self-worth.

Benefit: You stayed true to yourself by not allowing him/her to convince you to compromise your initial decision, which is an excellent example of using Self-Serving Strategies effectively.

Understanding and believing in your own self-worth is a very valuable measurement to have attained at such an early age. Congratulations!

#10.) You are in the eleventh grade and are currently preparing to take the Standardized Aptitude Test (S.A.T) to determine your score for college entrance. Your parents and high school counselor have stressed the importance of achieving a high score, since it may give you the advantage of attending the college of your preference. You want to do well, but you do not like feeling pressured. What are your options?

A.) You decide to study every chance you get, without taking any breaks to regroup and/or to relax. Studying begins to consume you and your brain is overwhelmingly on overload. You finally take the test, but you don't feel you did your best.
Consequence: Although you took the time to study seriously, you did not give your brain a chance to relax. You gathered a wealth of information by studying endlessly; however, your mind did not have the opportunity to process it properly. This may have attributed to the lack of confidence you displayed after taking the test. Learning how to balance your responsibilities with adequate rest and rejuvenation is an achievable goal. Please find time to have some fun the next time around. Sorry, but this is not an example of using Self-Serving Strategies.

B.) You decide to set-up a reasonable study schedule and follow it. You make it a point to set aside time to relax and rejuvenate your brain. You take the test with confidence and a positive attitude.
Benefit: You created and followed a plan of action that best suited your needs; thus practicing Self-Serving Strategies. Your efforts reflect your highest possible score, since you tried your absolute best. Congratulations on actively taking responsibility for your future.

C.) You decide to ignore the importance of this test. You become so pressured by what the results of this test may produce, that you develop a fear of failure complex. You procrastinate studying by having fun with your friends instead. You begin to lie to your parents about preparing for the exam. You are so scared, that you don't what to try. You take the test, but you know you did not do well because you were not prepared. You guessed at some of the answers to the confusing questions.

Consequence: You did as little as possible just to get by. You know you did not try your best, since you allowed fear to overtake reality. Fear of failure can be overcome by having a logical, attainable plan of action. Discussing your feelings with your parents and/or your high school counselor may also have been beneficial. Please seek help the next time feelings and emotions prevent you from trying your best, or even from trying at all. This is not an example of using Self-Serving Strategies.

This completes Chapter #7: The Eleventh Grade. I hope these examples of real-life scenarios have provided you with a practical approach of how to use Self-Serving Strategies effectively to benefit your future. Please consider using this concept now, as well as when you become a senior next year. Proficiently knowing all Six Bonus Fundamentals in Chapter #9: The Six Bonus Fundamentals may also provide you with valuable insight in creating positive future outcomes for yourself.

Chapter #8
The Twelfth Grade

Chapter #8 recognizes all twelfth grade seniors in high school with hope and promise. This year may be challenging for some of you, since the realization of goals previously set in your junior year may not materialize. Your original plans for your future may quickly be altered by one mindless and/or impulsive decision. It is imperative for you to stay focused on your goals this year, but it is also important for you to have fun. Please be advised that high school seniors are considered role models for the juniors, sophomores, and freshmen attending your school; therefore, your actions and decisions may directly affect others. Remember to make wise choices to ensure your safety and achievement of future goals.

The following ten examples vary in subject matter, which are intended to give you a wide spectrum of opportunities and possibilities that may provide you with growth and maturity beyond your years. Each example is equipped with three answer choices, along with a benefit and a consequence presented as a probable result; however, example #4-C lists a consequence and a benefit due to the explicit content and example #5-A also has both possible outcomes because of the plan of action taken in the decision. Please read with the intention of comprehending and using Self-Serving Strategies as a tool for the betterment of your future.

#1.) You are in the twelfth grade and your friends have introduced you to the concept of getting a tattoo. You have a lengthy discussion regarding this topic with your parents and they decide that you are old enough to make this decision on your own. Your circle of friends want to have the same design tattooed to signify unity within their group. You really want it because you want to be included in their group, but you want to know if there are any long term affects. What are your options?

A.) You decide to ignore your intuition that tells you to wait until you find out the information you are searching for and get the tattoo to be included with this group of friends. You feel included, but begin to recognize that this group doesn't share the same values that have been instilled in you by your parents. They begin to do things that make you feel uncomfortable and you have second thoughts about the symbol that is on your body that represents your affiliation with them.

Consequence: Your decision was made hastily; therefore, it may have long term affects for you because a tattoo is permanent artwork on your body. Although you may go to a doctor to get it removed, that area on your body may never be the same and it may hold a negative experience and/or memory for you. There also may be extra costs involved in the removal process that your parents may not be willing to pay for. This is not an example of Self-Serving Strategies because the decision may have adverse affects for you by not conducting the proper research before going forward.

B.) You decide to get as much information on the topic as possible, since your parents trust you to make an informed decision. You ask doctors about any health risks and removal procedures, if you change your mind after the fact. You conduct a survey of twenty people who have gotten tattoos within the last five years. The hardest question asked was "do you regret your decision to get a tattoo?" After gathering the data, you decide that getting a tattoo was not worth the possible long term affects that may occur. You are firm in your decision and are prepared to face alienation from this group.

Benefit: Because you did the research, you were able to make an informed decision that directly impacted you and your future. You stayed true to yourself by not giving in to peer pressure. By making this informed, adult decision, your parents may become more trusting of you. You have graduated from having novice decision-making skills to acquiring a level of maturity that is admirable, which is a great example of acquiring the power of self-definition. You also displayed Self-Serving Strategies in a proficient manner.

C.) You decide to get the tattoo, with no doubt in your mind. You are so happy because you are "in" with this group. But, you soon learn the real meaning of the symbol was to represent gang affiliation. Now, you have a tattoo and you are in a gang.

Consequence: You may be perceived very negatively by your school community and family for being associated with a gang. You may be expected to do things you know are wrong, but because you are in a gang you must cooperate; however, you have a choice to disassociate yourself from this gang, but it may be difficult and dangerous. For safety reasons, please ask for help before you alienate this group. Your grades may drop, which may change your college options. Your future may begin to look bleak. You now have a lot more issues to deal with that need to be addressed. This is an example of making a hasty decision because you rushed to get what you wanted without getting any information or facts beforehand. By exercising Self-Serving Strategies, you may have been able to identify characteristics in this group that may have deterred your choice.

#2.) You are in the twelfth grade and work after school and on weekends at a clothing store in the local mall. Your friends have visited you at work on many occasions and it has never interrupted your responsibilities. One night two close friends of yours came into the store to say "hi." This particular evening the sales floor was very slow, so the manager left early leaving you alone to close the store. Your friends knew the situation and ask if they could take some merchandise, since there was no one there to witness the theft. You know that this is wrong, but they have been your friends for a long time and you don't want to jeopardize sharing all the fun activities and events that take place senior year with them. What are your options?

A.) You decide to let your friends steal items from the store you were left in charge of. The next day at school your friends bragged about how they got free stuff from the store you work at. Frenzy emerged and you begin to feel overwhelmed with the demands of other students. The pressure got to you and you did not see any other way out, so you quit your job. You felt quitting was the only solution to the predicament you got yourself into because you did not know how to say "NO!"

Consequence: You quit your job, which means you eliminated your source of income. You proved that you do not currently have the confidence in yourself to voice your convictions and follow through with making the right decisions that may directly impact your future. Because you did not know how to say "No!," you exhibited traits of becoming a follower. Reviewing the main concept of Self-Serving Strategies as defined in the introduction of this book may help you learn how to acquire the power of self-definition, which may teach you how to focus on your future goals.

B.) You decide to say "no" to your friends and asked them to leave the store, so you can finish your work. The next day at school your friends seemed to display a negative attitude with you. You did not let their behavior influence a reaction from you; however, you continue to observe them for the next few days. You begin to notice their "give me" philosophy and reconsider their friendships. After careful thought, you decide to disconnect from associating with them. Over time, the friendships dissolve amicably.

Benefit: Your actions displayed a very mature attitude by knowing what was the right thing to do and then following through with it. You took it one step further by observing your "friends" in everyday situations and detecting patterns of behavior that you were uncomfortable with. By taking these proper steps, you stayed true to yourself and your belief system. You have not only practiced Self-Serving Strategies efficiently, you also acquired the power of self-definition.

C.) You decide to let your friends steal the merchandise from the store, with the understanding that it was a one time deal. You close the store as directed by the manager. Your friends did not mention the crime you all committed the night before to anyone at school the next day. You were not scheduled to work that afternoon; however, your boss called you in for a meeting. During the meeting, you quickly recognize the theft on a video tape the manager obtained from the security office. You are speechless, but your boss has a lot to say. Apparently, he/she was testing you to see if you were management material for an upcoming assistant manager's position. Because the video tape clearly indicated your involvement by giving your friends permission to commit the crime, you got fired on the spot. Your friends were notified that they are no longer allowed to enter the store, under any circumstance. The monetary value of the items stolen were calculated and deducted from your last paycheck.

Consequence: You got fired, which may have a negative impact for you when trying to seek employment in the near and foreseeable future. Because your boss understood that this was your first offense, he/she did not call the police to report the crime. Since you lost your source of income, you may need to make other arrangements to fulfill prior monetary obligations. You will need to tell your parents what happened. They may impose punishment and/or restrictions as another consequence for you to deal with. Anytime you decide to engage in any unlawful activity, please be aware that sooner or later you will get caught. The only good thing about this situation was that you were caught on your first offense, which instills a reality element that you can and will get caught. Please consider learning how to use Self-Serving Strategies by understanding its concept as defined in the introduction of this book. It may help you to make wiser choices that may affect your future in a positive manner.

#3.) You are in the twelfth grade and have had your driver's license for over a year. You have a car that you "fixed-up" to maximize speed and overall beauty. Although your car can reach a very high speed based on the engine you installed, you have never personally driven it to that limit. You also have no experience with any type of car racing. You have been "called-out" to race another senior who attends your rival school. You know street racing is illegal, but you have been challenged to a race that represents your school. What are your options?

A.) You decide to turn-down the offer to street race because you know just how dangerous it could be. You learn to deal with the "teasing" by instilling the "Bounce" method of coping with name calling and negative feedback. You walk proud with confidence in knowing you made the right choice for yourself.

Benefit: You stayed true to yourself by understanding how hazardous street racing may be and by not taking the risky chance of experiencing loss of life or serious injury for yourself or others. You gained a new technique called the "bounce" method, which helped you overcome the expected teasing factor that making an unfavorable decision may result in. You displayed leadership characteristics in this example, which may benefit you throughout all your future education and career endeavors. Congratulations on practicing Self-Serving Strategies and acquiring the power of self-definition. A full description of the "Bounce" method can be explored in Chapter #9: The Six Bonus Fundamentals for your review.

B.) You decide to take the challenge and you win the race. You are labeled a hero at school and you love the attention and popularity this notoriety has brought you. You enjoyed the "high" you got from this thrill seeking experience and want to explore other risk-taking adventures, since nothing bad happened the first time.

Consequence: This decision has given you a false representation that you are invincible, which may prove to be very dangerous for you and your future. If your thrill seeking adventures continue to escalate at a rapid rate, then you may never be safe and/or satisfied. You may eventually lose your lucky streak and this may result in life-changing events beyond your control or your desires. Examples may include, but are not limited to, being critically injured, disabled, or even dying from engaging in risk-taking behaviors. You may also injure or kill innocent people by your actions. Please consider understanding the concept of Self-Serving Strategies and begin to use it accordingly. You still have time to learn effective decision making skills that may benefit you and your future.

C.) You decide to take the challenge and get into a serious car accident that injures student bystanders and yourself. An ambulance takes you to the hospital and you are admitted in the intensive care unit. A few students are classified as critically injured and one person needs emergency surgery. Parents begin to arrive at the hospital and doctors discuss their child's prognosis with them. A few hours pass and your condition improves, so you are upgraded and transferred into a private room. The next day, you are notified that the student that received emergency surgery yesterday did not make it. You are solely responsible for the death of this person.

Consequence: You may be charged with legal action for the untimely death of the student that died. Your life may never be the same. Living with the fact that you are responsible for taking someone else's life is probably one of the hardest lessons you will ever have to deal with. This clearly exemplifies the importance of making the right choice when you are faced with a situation that involves risk-taking behavior that may result in life-threatening consequences. It takes a much stronger person to say "no." Please contemplate decisions more carefully in the future by practicing Self-Serving Strategies.

#4.) You are in the twelfth grade and have been invited to go to a party as a guest of a girl/guy you like. The party is at his/her house and the parents will be there. You have heard through the grapevine that his/her parents are considered "cool parents" because they allow co-ed sleepovers and provide alcoholic beverages at their parties for the teenagers. You really like this person and would love the opportunity to get to know him/her better. You know that underage drinking is a serious matter and that a co-ed sleepover is probably inappropriate for teenagers. You also know that your parents are not going to give you permission to attend this party if you tell them the truth. You want to go because you think it will be fun, but you know you would have to lie to your parents. What are your options?

A.) You tell him/her that you would not be able to make it because you know your parents will not give you permission to attend the party based on the truth. You are not willing to lie because you have built a trusting relationship with your parents, especially during your high school years. Although you like this guy/girl, you soon realize that he/she and his/her family do not share the same values yours does. You decide to stop exploring the chance of developing a romantic relationship with this person.

Benefit: You stayed true to yourself by focusing on your own best self-interest. You keep your strong, trusting relationship with your parents. You did not let peer pressure and/or temptation influence your decision to remain honest, which builds integrity and character traits favorable in adulthood. You may meet someone special in the near future that shares your values and beliefs, since you know what your standards are. This is an excellent example of using Self-Serving Strategies proficiently. Congratulations!

B.) You ask your parents if you can go and you clearly state that the parents of the guy/girl who invited you will be home during the party. You go and have a great time. The neighbors become bothered by the noise and call the police. The police arrive, assess the situation, and determine that underage drinking has occurred. Everyone is taken to the police station where all the teenager's parents are called to come pick them up. The parents responsible for the party who served alcoholic beverages to the teenagers are arrested. Your parents are very disappointed with the choices you made and ask you a direct question, "Did you know that the parents were going to allow drinking at this party?" You know you are in big trouble, so you answer truthfully.

Consequence: You broke the trust you have built with your parents over the past few years. Regaining their trust may take a long time. Punishment for this decision may be severe, since it is of utmost importance for your parents to get the message across to you that underage drinking is not only unlawful, it is also very dangerous. You may be entering college soon (if you chose education as your next goal step) and your parents may be more concerned about peer pressure and the temptation to drink alcohol. This is an example of lying by omission because you deliberately left out pertinent information from your parents that probably would have made a difference in their decision to let you attend this party. Please learn the concept of how to use Self-Serving Strategies correctly in an effort to make decisions for the betterment of your future.

C.) You ask your parents if you could sleep over a friends house, then go to the party instead. There are people at this party that you don't know, but you are willing to mingle with them. After a few drinks, you begin to feel light headed and decide to go to bed early. You are taken to the sleeping area and lay down. A few hours later, you are awoken by inappropriate touching and fondling. You were being sexually molested in your sleep by someone you just met. Fear overcomes you and you scream for help. Your parents are called and pick you up. You tell them everything.

Consequence: Your may experience adverse affects from this experience, so counseling is highly recommended for recovery and healing purposes. Your parent's priority is to help you cope with this traumatic ordeal; however, it may take them some time to trust you again. Although no one has the right to sexually abuse you in any manner at any time, you need to take responsibility for putting yourself in an unsafe environment in the first place. This was a clear example of just how important it is for parents to know exactly where their teenagers are, what they are doing, and with whom they are with. You clearly did not use Self-Serving Strategies when making this decision.

Benefit: You did display Self-Serving Strategies and acquired the power of self-definition, when you screamed for help and then told your parents the truth about what happened. Keeping this abuse to yourself may have prolonged the healing process, which may have influenced your future negatively. Bonus #1 in Chapter #9: The Six Bonus Fundamentals explains the importance of seeking help as soon as possible for the betterment of your future. Congratulations!

#5.) You are in the twelfth grade and have had a best friend for the last ten years. Your friendship has always displayed a healthy friendship pattern, as defined and described in "Friendship Wise" in Chapter #1: The Wise Segments. Recognizing that this is your senior year and you only have a few more months to spend with him/her, you want to make the most of it by creating meaningful memories. Recently you have become aware of different behaviors he/she has been exhibiting and you suspect that he/she may be experimenting with illegal street drugs. You are suspicious and want to ask him/her, but you don't want to jeopardize your friendship. What are your options?

A.) You decide to quickly assume that he/she is doing drugs, although you have no evidence of such activity. You bluntly accuse him/her of doing illegal street drugs and he/she explodes with anger. You get into an argument and he/she becomes violent with you. At first you react by fighting back and then you stop and walk away from the scene. He/she continues to yell at you as you leave. You suddenly realized that your friend's behavior is consistent with symptoms and reactions of drug use: anger, physical violence, verbal outbursts, and overall abusive actions. You then determine that this friendship is no longer healthy for you. Because you don't feel safe in communicating your decision with him/her, you avoid personal contact whenever possible. The message that you no longer want to be friends with him/her gets across over time. You go on with your life.

Consequence: By confronting your friend, you may have put yourself in a very dangerous situation if he/she was on drugs at the time. This assumption created a defensive reaction and violent outbursts that were directed to you. Please consider how important it is to keep yourself in a safe environment by evaluating the circumstance beforehand. Even if you did have evidence of him/her doing drugs, it would not have been a good idea to confront him/her. People who abuse drugs display very unpredictable behavior.

Benefit: When you realized how unsafe the situation was becoming, you quickly removed yourself from the environment without responding to the continued verbal abuse. Deciding to dissolve the friendship because you felt it had became unhealthy for you and the way you did it by keeping yourself safe, are examples of using Self-Serving Strategies effectively and acquiring the power of self-definition. Congratulations!

B.) You decide to watch your friend's behavior for a few weeks and determine that he/she is probably engaging in some type of drug activity. You are not willing to compromise your decision to live a drug free lifestyle, so you decide to have an open conversation with him/her. You clearly state your position and inform him/her that you are not comfortable with associating with anyone who is or might be doing drugs. He/she does not admit it, but becomes very defensive. You observe his/her attitude and decide to dissolve the relationship amicably because it no longer exhibits a healthy friendship pattern as described in "Friendship Wise" in Chapter #1: The Wise Segments.

Benefit: You stayed true to yourself and your belief system without accusing him/her of any wrongdoing. Not willing to compromise your values is a key component of acquiring the power of self-definition. Continuing your progression in this healthy manner may provide you with the skills to achieve your future educational and career goals. Congratulations on practicing Self-Serving Strategies proficiently.

C.) You ask your friend if he/she is doing drugs. He/she admits to smoking weed and offers you to try it after school. You know it is wrong and you have pledged to live a drug-free lifestyle, but you are curious and you don't think that trying it just once will drastically make a difference. You meet him/her after school and reluctantly try it. Your experience with smoking weed was quite pleasurable. You felt really relaxed because all your problems seemed minimal and unworthy of being worrisome. You continue to smoke weed on a regular basis because you really like the "high." You become an addict and your life is never the same.

Consequence: Your decision to try the drug and your justification for doing so caused the development of your addiction. Trying weed just once and enjoying the affects may convince you to continue doing it on a regular basis, thus becoming addicted. You may need to deal with this addictive behavior with counseling and support groups for the rest of your life. Your educational and future career goals may be compromised and unrealized because of the choices you have made. Please read "Addiction Wise" in Chapter #1: The Wise Segments for a review on the importance of diverting your curiosity to channel favorable outcomes that will benefit your future positively. This is not an example of using Self-Serving Strategies because you allowed curiosity to influence a decision you knew was wrong and you became addicted to smoking weed.

#6.) You are in the twelfth grade and are female. Your senior prom is approaching and you have a date, but do not own a formal dress to wear. Your parents are on a strict budget and can't afford to buy you a new dress; however, they have offered to purchase an inexpensive one from a second-hand consignment store. You don't have enough time to earn the money to buy a new dress yourself. You really want to go to your senior prom, but you are afraid of being embarrassed about wearing a used dress. What are your options?

A.) You decide not to go because you are overwhelmed with the possibility of being embarrassed. You simply do not want to take the chance of someone recognizing your second-hand dress. By not attending, you are guaranteed that you won't be humiliated or teased for not being able to afford a new modern dress.

Consequence: You forfeited your senior prom event because of something that might happen, which really means you let fear over power your decision. You also displayed low self-esteem by not believing in yourself to handle an uncomfortable situation, if it arose. People can't control how you feel about yourself. Only you can determine your self-worth and tolerance level for negative feedback. Knowing who you are and raising your self-esteem may provide you with the tools to make choices that may benefit you in a positive manner. This decision did hurt you because it eliminated the opportunity for you to create an experience that may have become a life-long high school memory. Your real friends may have missed sharing this milestone event with you. This is not an example of using Self-Serving Strategies because you allowed fear to overtake your judgment.

B.) You decide to go and take a chance of being noticed in a used dress. Someone does recognize the dress and makes it a point to embarrass you by telling other people. Word spreads throughout the crowd and the teasing begins. You get so upset with their behavior that you ask your date to take you home.

Consequence: You left early because you let others determine how you feel about yourself and the dress you were wearing. Your actions may have created a negative memory for yourself because reminiscing about your senior prom in the future may bring you sadness, anger, and more embarrassment. Learning the "Bounce" method as an alternative to dealing with teasing and embarrassing situations may provide a positive outcome in future encounters. A full description of the "Bounce" method can be reviewed in Chapter #9: The Six Bonus Fundamentals. This is not an example of using Self-Serving Strategies because you allowed others to influence your decision to leave. Learning how to acquire the power of self-definition means that you have the power within yourself to define who you are, without any negative influence by others around you. Please consider learning how to define yourself by practicing Self-Serving Strategies for the betterment of your future.

C.) You decide to buy a dress from the consignment store and tweak it to fit your fashion style and personality. You are proud of the creative alterations you made to your dress and are very excited to go to your senior prom. At the event, someone recognized the dress and asked you where you got it from? You stand tall and tell the truth. This person makes negative comments about it, but you hold your head up high, walk away without responding, and have a great time at your prom.

Benefit: You clearly know who you are and won't let anyone redefine your self-esteem with negative feedback. By walking away without any verbal communication, you empowered yourself and acquired the power of self-definition. You may have created a very memorable, positive experience for yourself. Congratulations on practicing Self-Serving Strategies by acknowledging your own power to self-define who you are.

#7.) You are in the twelfth grade and are a male. You have had the same girlfriend since ninth grade. She has just told you that she is twelve weeks pregnant. She waited to tell you because she did not want you to pressure her into having an abortion. She then tells you that the baby is in her body and that she has decided to have the baby, with or without your support. You were planning on attending college out of state after graduation and having a baby may make this goal nearly impossible to achieve. What are your options?

A.) You decide to go along with your plans and attend college out of state. You take on the responsibility of fathering this baby with your girlfriend by getting a part-time job and sending the money to her. You also decide to forgive her for her deceit. You remain in a committed relationship with her and come home during holiday and summer breaks. Your parents have also been supportive grandparents with the baby. Your decision to go out of state for school was solely based on future opportunities and not to escape from fatherhood pressure.

Benefit: You stayed true to yourself by realizing the best decision for your new family was for you to receive the best possible education that would benefit your future. This choice may give you opportunities to provide a healthy, stable family lifestyle. Although the sacrifice has been placed on your girlfriend to provide the full-time nurturing and daily caretaking of the baby, she has agreed to this commitment for the betterment of your new family's future. Marriage is an option, when the time is right for both of you. This is an example of using Self-Serving Strategies because your decision was handled with respect and responsibility and the outcome will benefit you and your family's future. This is a hard lesson learned; dealing with an unwanted pregnancy. Bonus Fundamental #3 in Chapter #9: The Six Bonus Fundamentals expresses the adverse affects for both males and females faced with this situation. Please review.

B.) You decide to change your plans and attend college near home on a part-time basis because you need to work full-time to support the baby. You forgive your girlfriend for her deceit and stay in a committed relationship with her. You soon realize that handling real-life responsibilities are hard work and you become overwhelmed. The stress has reached a level that is unbearable to manage and you seek help from a counselor.

Benefit: You did what you thought was best for you and your new family at the time. Attending school on a part-time basis to achieve your educational goals is an example of taking small steps to reach success. Although it will take longer to receive your college degree, completing it may provide job promotions and career opportunities that may definitely benefit your future in a positive manner. Perseverance is a wonderful character trait to acquire. When life became difficult to handle, you sought help with counsel. This is a mature way to deal with life's stressors. Congratulations on displaying Self-Serving Strategies by making a decision that best suited you and your new family. This is a hard lesson learned; dealing with an unwanted pregnancy. Bonus Fundamental #3 in Chapter #9: The Six Bonus Fundamentals expresses the adverse affects for both males and females in this situation. Please review.

C.) You decide that you can't handle the pressure of being a father and break-up with your girlfriend. You especially did not like the way she TOLD you what she was going to do, and the way she hid her pregnancy from you for three months. You tell her that a paternity test has to be taken to determine who the biological father is because you deny the validity of her accusation. In the mean time, you continue with your plans to attend school out of state after graduation. The baby is born and the test proved that the baby is in fact yours. You are mad and embarrassed, but it is your fear that overtakes your better judgment and you tell her that she is on her own; you abandon your baby. Later, you leave the state to attend college. Child support cannot be collected from you because you are a full-time student and do not have a job.

Consequence: You did not take any responsibility for your part in creating this baby. You caused your ex-girlfriend undue stress by denying the paternity, which was very hurtful to her. The anger you have for your ex-girlfriend has been redirected to your baby. This baby may not know his/her biological father, unless you decide to make the proper changes in your life that includes regular visitation and monthly child support payments. Bonus Fundamental #3 in Chapter #9: The Six Bonus Fundamentals exemplifies the fact that any sexual contact, with or without birth control, may result in an unwanted pregnancy. Please consider that the only 100% birth control that exists is total abstinence. This example is not using Self-Serving Strategies because your actions were very hurtful and you abandoned your baby, which is not taking responsibility for your involvement in creating this new life.

#8.) You are in the twelfth grade and have a good friend that has told you that he/she feels very pressured and depressed. He/she has communicated openly and honestly about wanting to commit suicide. He/she has also sworn you to secrecy. You are definitely stressed over this dilemma and are not sure just how to handle it. You know that telling someone is the right thing to do, but you have been sworn to secrecy. What are your options?

A.) You decide to keep your friend's secret and help him/her yourself. You spend all of your free time trying to convince him/her that life is worth living. Your schoolwork, homework, and after school activities become less important to you because you are focused on trying to keep your good friend alive; he/she commits suicide despite your efforts and sacrifice. You feel responsible for his/her death.
Consequence: Your heart was in the right place, but your plan of action consisted of your life being consumed by your friend's problems, which is not an example of a healthy friendship. You were not qualified to handle such a serious matter at hand and are not responsible for his/her death. People who are most affected by this death may try to push blame on you for not telling, but the ultimate decision to end his/her life was solely his/hers. Your

decision to help was not wrong; however, it is your civic responsibility to tell someone in life or death situations. A promise kept between friends can create a special bond; however, knowing when to break it displays real maturity and commitment to the friendship. You may experience feelings of guilt and remorse over this tragic incident. It is very important for you to seek help from a counselor, your parents, or a doctor to resolve those feelings and to learn how to deal with the loss of your friend. This is NOT an example of being "Friendship Wise," as defined and described in Chapter #1: The Wise Segments. This is not an example of using Self-Serving Strategies because you put yourself and your responsibilities last, which may have affected your future goals. Please take some time to heal and then move forward with your life.

B.) You decide to tell your school counselor what your friend told you. The counselor follows the proper protocol in dealing with suicidal students. Your friend receives the help and guidance he/she needs to overcome his/her suicidal thoughts. You went on with your own daily responsibilities, but you let your friend know that you were available if he/she needed you. At first your friend was mad that you broke your promise, but over time he/she thanked you for intervening to seek help.

Benefit: Although your friend swore you to secrecy, you knew telling someone the truth was the right thing to do. You displayed an example of being a healthy friend by being there for him/her, without allowing your life to become consumed by his/her problems. Learning boundaries and just how to balance what being a supportive friend really entails is essential in building healthy friendships. Congratulations on exercising Self-Serving Strategies in this life or death situation.

C.) You decide you don't want to lose your friend's trust or be labeled a "tattle tale," so you don't tell anyone. He/she commits suicide. Because you knew you should have told someone, you feel like it was your fault he/she died for keeping this life or death secret.

Consequence: You may have to seek counseling to heal from this tragic incident. Although friendship loyalty was an important aspect of your relationship, knowing when to disclose a secret (especially when life-loss is possible) for the betterment of the friend's well-being will always prevail. Life or death situations are not considered a tattle tale. It is definitely not your fault that your friend took his/ her own life; however, it is your civic responsibility to tell an adult as soon as any life-threatening information becomes available to you. Pease take all the time you need to heal, then move forward with your life and create a new plan of reachable goals. This is not an example of using Self-Serving Strategies because you failed your civic responsibility when you did not inform an adult of your friend's suicidal intentions.

#9.) You are in the twelfth grade and have recently discovered your attraction to the same sex. You have always otherwise been heterosexual. You are confused about your feelings and not sure how to explore them in a healthy manner to elude alienation and unnecessary teasing. What are your options?

A.) You decide to pretend that you are still attracted to the opposite sex and ignore all other feelings you have for the same gender. You continue to live your life as normally as possible because it is the easiest solution to your confusion.

Consequence: You chose a safe reason to remain heterosexual. It may be the easiest choice, but you did not stay true to yourself. Being who you really are and learning how to accept it are very important to your overall happiness and well-being. If you are really gay and don't explore your options of what that may mean to you, then you may be living a lie. Being alienated and/or teased by family members and/or close friends is a risk only you know when to take. Learning the "Bounce" method in bonus fundamental #3 of Chapter #9: The Six Bonus Fundamentals, may help you deal with negative influences that can arise if you choose to disclose your sexual orientation. Although you did not hurt anyone in the process, this is still not an example of using Self-Serving

Strategies because you may have hurt yourself by not exploring and understanding who you really are.

B.) You decide to ask for direction from your school counselor. He/she refers you to the school's psychologist on staff. You discuss your feelings with him/her and are encouraged to join a support group for teenaged gay and lesbians. In these meetings you are able to openly express your confusion in a safe environment. You begin to sort out your feelings and have come to a conclusion about your sexual preference in a partner.

Benefit: It does not matter if you are gay or not, you explored your options in a healthy manner. This choice also protected you from any unwanted, unnecessary teasing because your privacy and confidentiality was respected by the doctor and the support group. This is a great example of practicing Self-Serving Strategies. Remember, the best gift you can give yourself is being and accepting yourself for who you really are.

C.) You decide to begin a romantic relationship with someone of the same sex. You know that you are not sure of your intentions, but you convince this person you are gay and are very interested in pursuing a relationship with him/her. He/she takes your offer to get involved very seriously and you begin the process of getting to know each other. He/she starts to notice how uncomfortable you are in public, social situations and questions your sexual preference. You don't know how to respond because you are bewildered with the whole situation. He/she feels as though you are wasting his/her time and decides to end the relationship with you. He/she is hurt by your actions and feels used.

Consequence: Your choice caused an innocent person who was very comfortable with his/her own sexual orientation to experience hurtful feelings. The way you chose to explore your options and feelings was very unfair because you involved another person who may have had genuine feelings for you. This is in no way an example of exercising Self-Serving Strategies. Confusion and embarrassment needs to be addressed by you before you decide to engage in a romantic relationship with anyone. You may have lost a friendship because of your actions. Please explore personal struggles you may have with yourself in a healthier manner by seeking help from a professional counselor or doctor.

#10.) You are in the twelfth grade and graduation is upon you. Your classmates want you to participate in a prank at the graduation ceremony. A group of students is forming and they need your decision within the next week. The prank that is planned is not intended to harm anyone, but it will disrupt the ceremony while in progress. The purpose is to leave high school with an unforgettable "bang" that will keep people talking about your graduating class for years to come. You want to be remembered, but know it is rude, disrespectful, and inappropriate to interrupt officials conducting the ceremony. What are your options?

A.) You decide to join this group of pranksters and the plan runs smoothly. The prank was played out in the middle of the graduation ceremony and the audience laughed. No one was physically hurt, as planned and you know that you will be remembered for years to come. The officials did not appreciate the disruption and embarrassment it caused to them and the school. You were all caught in the act and will be disciplined accordingly.

Consequence: You knew that it was wrong, but you participated any way; therefore, you weren't being true to yourself. As punishment, you may be sanctioned for this prank under Chapter 19 rules and violations, which may include being arrested. Your diploma may also be revoked or delayed and/or the incident will be documented on your permanent school records, which may cause detrimental consequences for your college entrance next fall. It is your responsibility to acquire the power of self-definition by making decisions for the betterment of your future. Please learn how to use Self-Serving Strategies effectively and incorporate it into your daily lifestyle. People may talk about this prank for years to come.

B.) You decide to join this group of pranksters and everything goes wrong. The prank was not carefully executed and chaos occurred.

The person giving the speech at the time of the incident was so frightened by the unexpected prank that she fell back into the graduates sitting on the stage. This caused a domino effect as many people fell from their chairs onto the stage. The speaker was physically hurt, but did not sustain life threatening injuries and was taken by ambulance to the hospital as a precaution. Some classmates suffered minor injuries and were treated at the scene. A complete investigation was conducted and the graduation ceremony resumed after a two hour delay. You and your pranksters were not allowed to walk the graduation line and were removed from the venue. Because the prank failed, people may talk about it for years to come.

Consequence: You knew that it was wrong, but you participated any way; therefore, you weren't being true to yourself. As punishment, you may be sanctioned for this prank under Chapter 19 rules and violations, which may include being arrested. Your diploma may also be revoked or delayed and/or the incident will be documented on your permanent high school records, which may cause detrimental consequences for your college entrance next fall. You did not have the honor to walk the graduation line, which is a big disappointment for your family and friends that attended this event with anticipation and pride. Your actions caused an innocent person the undue stress and physical pain of experiencing an injury unnecessarily. You may be held partially responsible for his/her medical bills and punitive damages. Although your group did not have any intention of hurting anyone during this prank, you really cannot predict an outcome when you are planning to do something that is wrong to begin with. It is your responsibility to acquire the power of self-definition by making decisions for the betterment of your future. Please learn how to use Self-Serving Strategies effectively and incorporate it into your daily lifestyle. Congratulations! People may talk about this prank for years to come, but with negative reference.

C.) You decide to decline the offer because you want to ensure a guarantee that you will be able to participate in your graduation ceremony in its entirety. You do not inform the authorities of the planned prank, and the pranksters still go ahead with their plan of disruption. You will never forget about your graduation day because of the interruption and negative vibe the prank created.

Benefit: You did stay true to yourself by making a decision that clearly defined your values and purpose; thus acquiring the power of self-definition.

Consequence: However, because you did not inform the proper authorities of your knowledge of the prank, you did not fully practice Self-Serving Strategies. Your decision protected you from what you wanted, but it may have hurt innocent people in the process. It is very important to know that a tattle tale is when a person wants to deliberately get another person in trouble, so they tell anything and everything about that person; however, it is your civic responsibility to give an adult information that may cause the threat of danger or injury to others without fear of being labeled a tattle tale. Please consider using Self-Serving Strategies for its intended purposes and fully understand the definition beforehand.

This completes Chapter #8: The Twelfth Grade. Hopefully you have gained decision making skills that may directly impact your future in a positive manner by using Self-Serving Strategies proficiently. Grasping this concept may provide you with life skills essential in experiencing favorable outcomes on your next adventure; whether it be attending college or entering the workforce. Please read on to Chapter #9: The Six Bonus Fundamentals, as it may provide you with insight on living efficiently, which may also benefit your future endeavors.

Chapter #9
The Six Bonus Fundamentals

This chapter is devoted to providing the teenager with unsolicited advice in the form of six bonus fundamentals that are essential to live efficiently by enabling him/her to perform at optimum production levels. Living efficiently in this segment is defined as not having any unwanted negative memories that may cause flashbacks and limitations in your future plans. Because experience is stored in the memory bank of your brain, it is important to be aware of the consequences your actions may create.

Bonus Fundamental #1:
If you have ever experienced any type of unwanted sexual misconduct, the most important first step is to tell someone. If the first person you tell doesn't believe you, tell another. Keep telling your story until someone really hears what you are saying. Only after your testimony has been validated by an adult can you begin the healing process. This violation you have experienced, for whatever length of time, may have long term psychological impediments for you. Proper counseling and treatment will be beneficial for you, especially if explored in a timely manner. Your full potential about who you are and what you will become in the future may have been altered by this sexual abuse. This is the reason why coming forward at the onset of ANY MISCONDUCT is critical to the overall healing process. Remember, you are the product of your environment, but your experience does not have to equal to the sum of your life. You can change your future by healing from your circumstantial past, which is the best thing you can do for yourself; thus displaying Self-Serving Strategies.

Bonus Fundamentals #2:
If someone approaches you and offers you a drag of a cigarette, to consume an alcoholic beverage, or to intake any type of an illegal drug, simply say "No, Thank You." No other explanation is necessary and there is no reason to be rude. Then take a step back, turn

around, and walk away. By taking these two important steps, you have empowered yourself by displaying Self-Serving Strategies.

Bonus Fundamental #3

If someone teases you for any reason, or uses lazy language (name calling/profanity), you have the power to use the "Bounce" method to deal with this uncomfortable, negative feedback. At the onset of any discomfort, you may say "Bounce" and/or slap your lap, which may prevent any negativity from harming you before any seepage can occur. Basically, it's like building an invisible shield that protects you. Learning the "Bounce" method as an alternative to dealing with teasing and embarrassing situations may provide a positive outcome in your future encounters, which is best for you; thus practicing Self-Serving Strategies.

Bonus Fundamental #4:

If an unplanned pregnancy comes into your life, you may never be the same no matter what your decision is. Both males and females suffer adverse affects from an unplanned pregnancy, despite the outcome. For example, if you plan on having the baby, your educational goals and financial obligations will change. Becoming a parent is a huge responsibility that requires commitment, maturity, and self-sacrifice. If you decide on having an abortion, you may always wonder about that child that you did not bring to full term. Adoption may also bring a whole other set of emotions that you may not be aware of at the time of your decision. For example, you might wonder for the rest of your life what happened to that child you gave up. Because a 100% birth control option does not currently exist, except for complete abstinence, please consider the possibly of an unwanted, unplanned pregnancy happening every time you engage in any type of sexual contact. Having sex is very complex. If you and your partner decide on having a sexual relationship, knowing and fully understanding the responsibilities and consequences that may result in adult behavior beforehand may enable you to make a well informed decision that suits the both of you. Having sex does not equate maturity. Knowing and doing what is right for you by not giving into peer pressure and temptation may provide you with growth and maturity over time; thus displaying Self-Serving Strategies.

Bonus Fundamental #5:

If there is only one thing you learn from this book, I hope it's the fact that love and sex are two separate things other than the fact that sex is tangible and love is intangible. Although they intertwine, each has its own meanings and reasons for existing. Sex is a physical act that is based on an emotional connection that you share with another person with whom you trust, respect, and love. Sex should not be treated as a game to be played by getting someone to love you, nor is it a requirement for you to prove your love for another person. When you really love another human being, you would be willing to do anything for that person, within healthy means. For example, if your boyfriend/girlfriend had gotten into a car accident that left him/her in a wheelchair for the rest of his/her life, would you be able to accept the fact that this circumstance may affect your life if you choose to continue the relationship? Ask yourself, "Do I truly love my boyfriend/girlfriend enough to accept the consequences and challenges that have been put before us?" To love another human being is to take full responsibility for that person in good times, but most importantly, to provide support in the most challenging of times. Knowing who you truly are as a person will help you to realize what your limitations are, if any, when it comes to fully committing yourself to another human being. Love is a wonderful thing, if engaged in a healthy manner. Self-evaluation is a key step in practicing Self-Serving Strategies.

Bonus Fundamental #6:

Learning the basic Universal Law of give and take will provide you with insight into the way the world works. People have different terms, definitions, and interpretations for this concept. Basically, it is the belief that what you put out in the atmospheric universe will return naturally to you, but in a different form. For example, if you do something terrible to a person, then something negative will come your way in your future. It is not always clearly recognizable because the negative influence will be disguised and it may happen when you least expect it. To elaborate, if you did something to someone today, something bad may not necessarily happen to you tomorrow. It is also very important to fully understand that the negative repercussions will not come from the same person you harmed. If the person you harmed retaliates against you, then this is revenge and not the laws of the universe completing its cycle. If you think about it as creating half circles in the universe, with your actions representing the bottom half and the universe completing the circle with the top half with either a negative or positive force, then you may be able to envision it accurately and properly. Always doing the right thing, which includes not posing any negative actions upon another person, will benefit your future in a positive manner by completing positive circles in your realm; thus practicing Self-Serving Strategies.

Chapter #10
Conclusion

In summation, by practicing Self-Serving Strategies you may be able to retrain the part of your brain that influences decision making, which directly impacts your life and future. Each day is an opportunity that brings you closer to your ultimate, desired goal. It is also very important for you to know that mistakes or taking a detour from your goal's path does not necessarily equate failure. Sometimes redirection and modification of an original plan may end in a better result, since experience and perseverance are also invaluable life lessons to acquire.

You have the power within yourself to make great things happen in your future. So, go ahead and amaze yourself with what all you can accomplish. You really do have your future at your fingertips. Plan accordingly and use your time wisely.

Thank you so much for reading *Teen Wise* It is my hope that you will utilize the concept you have learned when faced with difficult situations and everyday challenges. I wish you the absolute best in achieving all your dreams and goals. Believe in yourself, as I believe in you.

Ms. Celeste

LaVergne, TN USA
31 August 2009
156463LV00002B/3/P